THE COLLABORATION EFFECT

Overcoming Your Conflicts

MICHAEL A. GREGORY

Published by Michael Gregory Consulting, LLC

Distributed by Bublish, Inc.

Paperback ISBN: 978-1-64704-267-7
eBook ISBN: 978-1-64704-266-0

*I thank God, my supportive family
and friends, and especially my wife, Roma.*

PREFACE

This guide is written for leaders to be more focused on the tasks at hand, provide them with confidence when navigating difficult situations, and result in more peace in professional and personal relationships. Leaders may be at the executive level, midlevel managers, front line supervisors, team leads, or those who have to lead in a given situation. Having been in all of these situations, this text is written for those that lead and want to lead.

It is great to be a member of a team when everyone is aligned and moving in the same direction. When everyone is aligned, there is a sense of compassion, generosity, hope, humility, joy, kindness, and peace amid the group. By comparison, being a member of a team where there are those with big egos, false pride, greed, envy, lies, resentment, and sense of superiority is no fun. Working with futurists, innovators, neuroscientists, and numerous successful individuals, I have pored over thousands of blogs, articles, books, links, and Internet commentaries. In this book I hope to share what I have learned on various topics, such as collaboration, emotions and empathy, health, negotiations, relationships, technology, and workplace culture.

There are common threads among these items. We all look for ways to minimize pain and maximize outcomes. Or looking at it differently, eliminate obstacles and arrive at a solution. We look for ways to do this personally and professionally. Praying for guidance and giving this tremendous thought, I came to the conclusion that helping others to experience a sense of fulfillment, joy, and success at work and home would be rewarding for me. Over my many years of my professional life with various life experiences, I have gained happiness and success from the lessons I have learned. I would like to share these with you.

The Collaboration Effect® is a registered trademark and is a proprietary system that I developed to enhance relationships, resources, and revenue. The process is fundamentally about building relationships [or connecting with others], listening actively, and educating judiciously to build bridges to negotiate closure.

Working with neuroscientists for more than five years, I explored brain scans with medical doctors, conducted research, blogged more than 250 weekly posts, networked with experts, and wrote other books related to this topic such as *Peaceful Resolutions* and *The Servant Manager*. These have all shaped the commentary in this book. I want to especially thank Dr. Erika Garms, author of *The Brain Friendly Work Place*, Dr. John B. Molidor, Professor at the Michigan State University Medical School, and Dr. Rick Hanson, with the Greater Good Science Center at the University of California -Berkeley

Throughout my career, I have conducted more than 2,500 mediations and negotiations professionally and as a volunteer. Those for corporations have money at stake. These mediations and negotiations ranged from nearly $1 billion (with Fortune 100 companies and boards of directors) to tens of thousands of dollars with small businesses. I have volunteer mediated nearly monthly for more than 16 years in housing court, conciliation court, in public housing disputes, with neighborhood disputes, and between gangs. As you can see, I have a passion for conflict resolution and for promoting collaboration. All of these elements have helped shape this book.

While connecting relationships, listening actively, and educating judiciously for collaboration is necessary as a foundation, it is possible to proceed to another level. Typically, a mediator or negotiator works to co-create, build bridges, and negotiate win-win solutions with others. Of course, along the way, we typically must work with difficult people and overcome conflict. There is no panacea. Given the human condition, we have to realize this and address these concerns. It's not about me. It's all about we. But *we* starts with *me*. In the end, if the other party does not want to work with you, don't take it personally. Rather, accept it and move on.

My hope is that this commentary will be a ready reference and tool to help you work with others in a positive and constructive manner. The lessons learned here can be applied at work as well as in your personal life.

I would like to thank my C-Suite (CEOs, COOs, CFOs, CIOs) friends, and my many other friends, associates, and colleagues that offered their insight and encouragement, and my publisher Bublish and, in particular, Kathy Meis for her very thoughtful and helpful comments. I also want to thank Dr. Sally Kohlstedt for invaluable insights and comments. Most importantly, I would like to thank my amazing, understanding wife, Roma.

TABLE OF CONTENTS

The Collaboration Effect is all about **connecting** relationships, **listening** actively, and **educating** judiciously in order to build bridges to negotiate closure.

AN OVERVIEW

The Collaboration Effect® is based on neuroscience and is all about connecting relationships, listening actively, and educating judiciously in order to build bridges and negotiate closure. The text begins with a story based on a real-world example of an actual event to demonstrate the process and introduce you to how powerful this process can be even in a very difficult situation with someone thought to be very difficult to work with. This story sets the stage for the text as details are explained on how to use and apply The Collaboration Effect.

The first three chapters explore what collaboration is and why it matters, present a framework for win-win outcomes, and align social skills with difficult people. After all we all have had to work and live with some people that we may find difficult to interact with. In chapter four you are introduced to the three key elements of The Collaboration Effect: connecting relationships, listening actively, and educating judiciously. In chapters five, six, and seven these three elements of The Collaboration Effect are elaborated on in detail to give you what you need so that you can take action and apply it at work and home. The last chapter focuses on how to build bridges to negotiate closure. After all what you want is to negotiate closure and move on to the next item on your agenda or the next opportunity.

Not every difficult situation with others can be resolved. Sometimes it is best to accept differences and move on, or to pursue legal avenues and have someone else (a trier of fact, an arbi-trator, or a jury) make the decision. However, as a mediator with over 2,500 experiences, I offer you insights so that you can work with others to overcome conflict, and work collaboratively to find solutions. The goal is "something you both really appreciate", but sometimes the end result is "something you both can only accept". If you want to overcome conflict or you know someone that is in conflict with someone else this book on The Collaboration Effect may help you or them with that conflict. If you are in business and you want to enhance relationships, reduce rework, avoid mental toil and physical pain, avoid wasted resources, and enhance revenue and the bottom line this text will help you.

Each chapter has at least one story. They help bring home key points based on real world experiences. Each chapter has at least one call out of something important that may truly change your life if you implement it by taking positive action going forward. The purpose of this text is to help make the world a better place by promoting collaboration, resolving conflicts, and working towards closure in negotiations.

A STORY TO
SET THE STAGE

T he commentary that follows is based on a real world set of facts that have been altered for confidentiality reasons. This story brings home the application of the three elements of The Collaboration Effect. These are

1. Connecting relationships,
2. Listening actively, and
3. Educating judiciously

in order to build bridges to negotiate closure.

Background

A business valuation appraiser of closely held businesses contacted me and told me an attorney would be calling me regarding a case in which he was an expert. The attorney called and told me there were six attorneys on a team representing a wealthy estate. The attorney told me he was the lead attorney, billing at $1,000 an hour. He had a plan that he wanted to share with me and he wanted to know how I could help him. He was very sure of himself as a litigating attorney that specialized in tax controversy issues for wealthy clients.

He indicated that the appraiser gave him an appraisal for a technical issue in a valuation at between 30% and 35%. The firm used 30% on the tax return. After an initial call with an IRS agent that was auditing this case, the agent indicated that he thought the right number was probably 10% for the issue. There was also a small legal issue. The lead attorney indicated that he was going to tell the IRS agent (who was also an attorney) why the agent was wrong regarding the valuation issue, and also write a 40-page brief telling the agent why the agent was wrong with the legal issue as well. After that the attorney indicated the case would be unagreed and he anticipated his law firm would represent the client, take the case to Appeals at the IRS, and settle the case there. Then he asked me, "What could you do to help me?" I thought for a moment and then I responded, "If this is the approach you want to take, I can't help you." There was a pause on the other end of the call, and then he asked me very much as a matter of fact, "What would you do?" I indicated in a nutshell that he needed to "connect with the agent to develop a rapport, listen actively with the agent to understand how he determined the 10%, and educate the agent judiciously to resolve the issue with the IRS at this level." He asked me to go on.

Connecting Relationships

I indicated that he needed to build trust with the IRS agent and learn everything he could about the agent before getting into the issues. I suggested doing research on the internet with various sources of social media to learn everything he could about the IRS agent. Perhaps this could be done by one of his staff members. I also suggested that he network with others at the law firm and outside the firm. As the lead attorney, I felt that he needed to build trust with the IRS agent by being honest, straightforward, open, and accepting. That was my emphasis. The attorney asked for some help in that regard, so I helped him with the kind of small talk and open-ended questions to ask to initiate a conversation before diving into the issues. We talked about this for about an hour to help him to be able to ask about 15 minutes of questions with the IRS agent. I suggested this approach, "Before going further why don't you ask him something like this: 'You know we have to work together on this case. I think it would be helpful to build some trust. If you are ok, I would like us to each share some background with each other so we could get to know more about each other. Would you be amenable to this?' Assuming he says yes, why don't you ask him if you can ask him some questions first. When a person has been listened to, they are more receptive to listening to the other party. This will help with the process."

Then the lead attorney asked me what kinds of questions he should ask. I suggested questions like this:

- "Where did you go for undergrad?
- Where did you go to law school?
- Where are you from originally?
- Where do you live now?
- What do you like to read?
- Where do you like to go for vacation or a getaway?
- Do you have any pets? If so what kind of pets?
- Are you a morning or afternoon person?
- What do you like to do for fun?
- Do you drink coffee? If so, what kind do you like?"

And some other questions, but you get the idea. The lead attorney asked me how long he should ask these and follow up type questions. I suggested something like 15 minutes for both his questions and those from the IRS agent. However, I suggested asking questions and listening to the agent for the vast majority of the time was preferred. He agreed to give it a try.

A couple of weeks later I received a call from the lead attorney. He indicated that he had contacted the agent. I asked him how it went. He said, "surprisingly well." I asked him to share with me what happened. He indicated he asked the agent what we had discussed and the IRS agent was responsive to the conversation. With that the lead attorney asked a host of questions and found some facts including:

The agent

- Went to Boston College for undergrad.
- Went to Boston University for law school.
- Was originally from Boston.
- He now lives in Boston.
- I like to read espionage and historical mystery.
- For vacations I like to travel, but for get aways I like to escape to northern New Hampshire.
- He has two dogs.
- He is a morning person.
- He is a runner and he enjoys running with his dogs.
- He maintains a healthy life style.
- He drinks coffee and prefers Starbucks coffee.

These were some of the major findings among other things.

I asked how long the small talk lasted. The lead attorney said he was looking at his watch. After 15 minutes he switched over to the legal issue. He was very surprised, but in about another 15 minutes they resolved the legal issue and now there was no need for the 40-page brief.

From there, the lead attorney indicated he would get back to the IRS agent in a week or two to set up a meeting to discuss the valuation issue. That is what he wanted to discuss with me. I suggested that this needed to be a pleasant, quiet place conducive to conversation.

I suggested we think of this as three periods with connecting relationships, listening actively and educating judiciously before trying to bridge differences to negotiate closure. The lead attorney asked me "What would you suggest?" I asked him, "How long do you think the meeting should last on the valuation issue?" The lead attorney responded, "about an hour". Then I suggested, "let's set it up for two hours to not have any time constraints and to allow plenty of time for a bathroom or a refreshment break." He agreed. I suggested, "With the IRS agent being a morning person, what do you think about setting up the meeting for 9 AM?" He concurred.

The law firm had a very nice office overlooking Boston Harbor, so I liked the lead attorney's idea of meeting there. I suggested instead of having six attorneys attend from the firm that the meeting only have the lead attorney and one other attorney. Experts have suggested the other attorney be engaging. The two of you will meet with the IRS agent. The other attorney was there for small talk at the beginning and to take notes. We all look for food, water, shelter, and sex. We need to address these needs. The other attorney will listen and engage with the IRS attorney.

Providing relationship enhancing snacks keyed to the other party's preferences is helpful. Regarding food and water, brain friendly food is a good choice. Borrowing from Dr. Erika Garm's book, The Brain Friendly Workplace[1], I suggested antioxidants, chocolate, peanut butter, and some other things[2]. To remain hydrated, have water and Starbucks coffee. Donuts and bagels are not recommended. The food and beverages should be placed on the side or perhaps a counter, ahead of time. A reasonably small round table was perfect for three people. When the IRS agent entered the room the lead attorney offered both food and beverages to the IRS agent and introduced the IRS agent to the other attorney. The intention is to be sociable.

The IRS agent may take some coffee or bottled water, but likely will not take any of the food offered initially. I suggested that the lead attorney and the other attorney initiate taking food so that the IRS agent would feel comfortable joining them possibly, and smell the dark chocolate and/or peanut butter. This was done to appeal to the senses. The first half hour or so would focus on small talk. Even though the second attorney was thoroughly briefed, the second attorney's role was to not reveal that information. Rather the second attorney was there to encourage the IRS agent to share his story. Rather the goal was to understand him and to build trust.

Listening Actively

The second period focused on listening actively. Now the emphasis would be on asking how the IRS agent came up with 10% for the valuation issue. The questions needed to be without judgment. The emphasis was to listen actively by summarizing, paraphrasing, asking open ended questions and empathizing. Empathizing involves identifying with the IRS agent, understanding what is involved with his analysis, relating to the IRS agent, and genuinely finding out his point of view. The idea is to build rapport with the agent. There are no judgments with respect to the analysis presented. This too was set up for about 30 minutes, but in reality, it took slightly less time. At this point it was suggested to take a break. There was a short 10-minute break when each of the participants took some of the snacks, obtained some fluids, and took a short bathroom break. There was some small talk related to his dogs and running, since the second attorney was also a runner and ran with his dogs.

This led into summarizing the second period in order to lead into the third period. Before proceeding the lead attorney was able to summarize the issue from the IRS agent's perspective. The IRS agent commented that the lead attorney summarized the key points even better than he had, himself.

Educating Judiciously

In the third period the lead attorney presented additional commentary and facts. He was very well-prepared. We had worked together on how to present this information as to educate rather than to intimidate the IRS agent. He and his team had done their homework. There is an IRS Job Aid on the issue. It turns out his appraiser had used nine of 32 possible areas of consideration from the IRS Job Aid when developing his valuation percentage that ranged from 30% to 35% on this issue. Upon further analysis eight of the remaining areas of consideration also had applicability to the facts in the case. The lead attorney presented the additional facts in each instance and then he asked the IRS agent if he concurred with the IRS Job Aid that given these facts, each of these facts tended to increase the valuation percentage. After each of the eight facts was presented and discussed the IRS agent said, "yes" this would tend to increase the percentage. This is very important. Every time the other side sincerely believes and states "yes", this helps move that person closer to your perspective. After about a half an hour having gone over all eight areas, it was time to move into the potential negotiation stage.

Beginning the Negotiation

Working with the lead attorney, a very specific question had been drafted ahead of time to reach out to the IRS agent. The lead attorney stated, "With our original expert appraiser's appraisal he indicated the valuation issue should be between 30% and 35% for tax filing purposes. We put 30% on the return. You had indicated that you thought the appropriate number before today's session should have been 10%. From our additional research using the IRS Job Aid, we presented facts and you concurred that the eight items brought up would tend to increase the valuation percentage. We now think the right valuation percentage should be 35%. However, before we go any further what do you think?" The IRS agent thought for a few moments, paused and then he said, "Would you accept 34%?" The lead attorney graciously accepted the offer and the parties drafted an agreement that could be finalized after the meeting.

Shortly after the meeting I received a call from a very happy lead attorney. He could not believe what happened in this case. The negotiation had shifted the situation from owing the IRS $1.6 million to the IRS providing his client a $400,000 refund on tax previously paid with the return. He was so excited he asked if I could fly to Boston at some point in the future to speak to his firm and to share what we had done. A few months later I did exactly that and I spoke to about half of the attorneys at that firm. Some of those in attendance had gone to Harvard Law School. Given their backgrounds, I received an invitation to make a presentation at the Harvard Club in Boston and then a couple of years later, I was invited back again to give a similar presentation.

The Collaboration Effect of connecting relationships, listening actively, and educating judiciously to build bridges to negotiate closure really works. It takes planning, the right attitude, appropriate, enthusiastic buy in, and dedication to make it work. It doesn't just happen. This example demonstrates how it actually worked in real life and how it can work for you.

Now let's get started so that I can help you learn how to apply the key points of this story based on this real-world example.

Chapter 1

COLLABORATION AND WHY IT MATTERS

"None of us is as smart as all of us."
—Ken Blanchard

Collaboration is a relatively simple idea, but it is different than communication. Whereas communication is an exchange of information, collaboration requires working with someone with the intention to create something. There is a common goal when you collaborate.

Collaboration is good for the bottom line, customer satisfaction, employee engagement, training and development, and leadership development. All stakeholders can potentially win when collaboration is working effectively. Our underlying psychological needs are what plays out when dealing with conflict constructively and working towards collaboration. The benefits of collaboration in the workplace and the process of creating a more collaborative environment provide many benefits that help us. Neuroscientist refer to this as minimizing pain or maximize reward.[3] In business it is often referred to minimizing pain or maximizing outcomes.

What Are the Benefits of Collaboration in the Workplace?

Studies demonstrate that by focusing on collaboration, customer satisfaction, and employee engagement, companies can improve their bottom line and outcomes. When we pool ideas and skill sets, we provide better outcomes for customers and employees feel valued. This enhances business growth. Here is a list of rewards when collaboration takes place. Clearly there are many benefits associated with collaboration.

- Increased productivity
- Better communication
- Open innovation
- Faster response to market opportunities
- Increased efficiency
- Enhanced employee satisfaction
- Improved retention
- Quicker closure
- Shared ideas
- Faster employee development

Why do companies focus so much on the bottom line and not fully explore the power of collaboration? Schools of business focus on the bottom line. After all, if you cannot meet the bottom line, you can't stay in business. At the same time our educational system has changed and now clearly promotes better outcomes and working collaboratively towards our goals. In fact, today, the best schools focus on collaboration[4], helping their students learn a valuable new skill set. Can we, as a society, learn from our educators? I think the answer is yes. The next generation has a broader focus on collaboration and sustainability, the environment, and global social wellbeing. By making the decisions about more than the bottom line, listening to each other, and focusing on the tactics used to overcome conflict and promote collaboration, produces significant positive results in all areas. Today, rapidly growing, successful firms that attract the best people focus not only on the bottom line, but also on ethics and a global perspective.

As a negotiator, you can be the hero when you facilitate collaboration. Not all negotiations are successful, but when they are and when everything comes together, it can be very rewarding. A successful negotiation can significantly enhance your reputation within your company, with vendors and customers, and with other stakeholders[5].

Once employees notice that their leader is willing to collaborate, they will be inspired to collaborate more often with others, too. It will become part of your culture to work with one another, watch out for each other, and work towards common goals. As I mentioned earlier, this has big benefits for an organization, so executive teams are looking for leaders who understand the power of collaboration.

> A successful negotiation can significantly enhance your reputation within your company, with vendors and customers, and with other stakeholders.

With the advent of artificial intelligence[6], it is clear that being creative, flexible, and social are key human skills for the future. Communication and collaboration are needed now and even more so in the future. What can you do to enhance your skills now? An executive once stated, "I ask my employee what skills do you need to enhance now for your next position and for five years from now? More than likely, the position does not even exist today." What he was asking is what technical skills, social skills, behavioral skills, communication skills, conversational skills, and other important elements will you need in the future, and what steps are you taking to enhance your current skill set? This question makes one think. Today, soft skills (referred to as the critical skills today) on such topics as leadership, understanding yourself and others, communicating effectively, enhancing effectiveness, managing diversity, managing your time and your life, collaboration, and building engaged workgroups matter more than ever. Take a look at your current skill set and ask yourself what skills you need to enhance for your next position.

Why Should Organizations Choose Collaboration Over Competition?

Wait a minute. Isn't competition good in the workplace? Isn't competition what makes our nation great? The question really is, what is healthy competition that will promote collaboration with your team? When we collaborate as a team, stay focused on the goal, and have each other's backs, we all do better. The group is only as good as the weakest link in the chain. When the chain breaks, we all fail. You might have one super link in the chain, but that does not matter when the chain breaks. By shoring up your weakest link, the entire chain is stronger. This often means prioritizing collaboration over internal competition.

There's nothing wrong with a little healthy competition, but it can also get out of hand. Competition can create a negative culture where people do not feel valued. What are some signs that your corporate culture might need to tone down competition?

- Backstabbing
- Distrust
- Infighting
- Hoarding of people, intelligence, and IT
- Less sharing of people, intelligence, and IT
- Intelligence becomes power
- Credit becomes the name of the game
- Turnover
- Decreased productivity

I worked for an organization that kept their eye on the ball, remained ethical, promoted healthy competition, but had to internally compete with another part of the organization that had lost its way. Our part of the organization played by the rules. There was a balance between customer satisfaction, business results, and employee satisfaction. We had good management. The home office began to place more and larger demands on the organization (does this sound familiar?). Our organization kept us informed and explained why we needed to work smarter to address the changing competition in our overall environment.

Competition was intense for resources. Headquarters decided who received resources (training, supplies, hires, promotions, and other important tangible and intangible items). The other part of the organization as it turns out began to cut corners on quality, and provided reports that we could not believe. We could not understand how they could possibly be doing what they were presenting to headquarters with their periodic reports. We were told we were not being as efficient by headquarters. Why couldn't we meet the goals of our internal competitor? We didn't know why either. We were trying to understand, but the information was not being shared by them.

Then at one point the facts came out. Customers did not appreciate the lower quality and they began to complain. It was clear the quality issues were from the other part of the organization. Then it was discovered that there were some accounting irregularities and that some information submitted was fabricated. Headquarters launched an internal investigation. Some top level and mid-level people were terminated and some demoted for not having raised an internal alarm about what was going on. This was clearly an example of an unhealthy competition within an organization. After that the organization was reorganized. Balanced measures were structured to consider business results, customer satisfaction (external vendor focus groups with clients) and employee satisfaction (major vendor internal polls). Yes, the organization wanted to meet the bottom line, but they also wanted employees that operate with corporate culture shared values.

Conversely, collaboration can create a positive climate in your organization—one where innovation can thrive. Here are some of the positive benefits of collaboration:

- Breakthrough results
- A common vision
- A shared sense of responsibility
- Customer satisfaction
- Trust
- Straightforwardness
- Openness
- Acceptance
- Responsibility
- Engaged employees
- Improved bottom line

One positive way to promote healthy competition and collaboration is to encourage a healthy rivalry between teams. This can promote positive benefits for an organization. When a team is aligned, it makes for a very healthy work environment. The team knows that in the end, everyone wins as part of the team. Everyone will reap the benefits of working on the selected winning idea. The best practices will be shared with everyone. In a healthy competition to find workable solutions, the team members are all aligned working towards the same goal.

You want your organization to nurture an environment where people can be straightforward, honest, transparent, open, responsible, and accepting of one another. Team members should know that when mistakes are made, apologies are offered and accepted. Participants separate the people from the process. In other words, participants should be tough on the problem and gentle on the people involved.

The team knows that it can count on everyone to put forth their best effort. All participants honor their commitments to the team. If problems arise, they should be brought to the attention of the team leader as soon as possible. This enables the team to assess what might be appropriate going forward. This is why collaboration works better than competition.

As young people, we are taught to work hard, study hard, and do our best. If we do this, we are told that we will get ahead. Then, when the best technician becomes a manager, all of that is turned on its head. Why? Because a manager is rewarded not by how well he or she performs, but by how well *the team* performs. The manager is rewarded for being able to transfer skills and help others be the best they can be. The manager's goal is to help the team function at top efficiency and effectiveness. A strong manager recognizes that everyone on the team has unique skills and characteristics that they bring to the team. By bringing the skills of a diverse team together, the entire operation can improve.

What Does it Take to Promote Collaboration?

Ideally, it starts at the top. For a group, that may mean you if you are the group manager or team lead. For a mid-level manager, that may mean you and your managers. For an executive, it probably means working with the organizational leadership team.

When everyone is aligned and engaged, corporate cultures begin to change for the better. Why because the mantra changes from, "It's all about me!" to "It's not about me. It's all about we. But we starts with me." This is an underlying theme of this book.

> "It's not about me. It's all about we. But we starts with me." This is an underlying theme of this book.

It is up to us to work together, do the right thing, do what it takes, and have fun along the way.

After all, we don't want to take ourselves too seriously. Here are some ways that you can promote collaboration as a leader in your organization:

- Promote ethical leadership that demonstrates that collaboration is truly valuable.
- Incorporate collaborative behaviors into performance evaluations.
- Set aside time to build and foster relationships.
- Listen and promote listening with open-ended questions to bring others into the process.
- Engage project managers that focus on building strong, cross-functional teams by recognizing and rewarding those who demonstrate best practices and behaviors.

Wouldn't you like to work in a more collaborative environment? Other professionals and various studies have shown[7] that the keys to a more collaborative environment abide in these three principles: diversity, equality, and focus. It takes effort in all three of these areas and an intention to embrace collaboration, to start to change a competitive or even a hostile environment into a collaborative one. Let's take a look at all three principles:

> **Diversity** - When we use the term diversity, we need to explore three levels: diversity of primary visible attributes; diversity of below-the-surface characteristics; and diversity of tertiary attributes, which we are often not aware of unless we dig a little deeper. Primary visible attributes include race, age, ethnicity, physical abilities, and sometimes sexual orientation. These clues are often used for quick evaluation, but they can also lead us astray by ascribing stereotypes.

Visible attributes can be misleading. We all have implicit bias. This bias is shaped by our life experiences, what we have been taught, and what we have chosen to reinforce. Exploring our own diversity and the diversity of others can broaden our understanding. Taking advantage of different points of view can lead to a better corporate culture, allows for more innovation, and by its very nature better business results, customer satisfaction, and employee satisfaction.

Below-the-surface characteristics are things like religious beliefs, nationality, geographic location, marital status, parental status, education, income, work background, and military experience. We generally cannot see these characteristics, though indicators like a wedding ring on the left ring finger is likely to indicate someone is married and certain clothing can indicate a person's religion. Tertiary attributes include such things as learning style, personality type, emotional intelligence, conversational intelligence, bias, and professional orientation. Does your company recruit for all levels of diversity? Is your work environment inclusive of others?[8] The more we explore and celebrate diversity, the greater the likelihood of creating an environment of understanding and collaboration. By accepting others and their insights, we open ourselves up to additional ideas and ways to see the world. By accepting diverse ideas, it is possible to expand our thinking and have a better, higher quality result in our work.

Equality - Neuroscientists present us with the
SCARF model, which stands for status, certainty,
autonomy, relationship, and fairness. David Rock
pioneered the SCARF model in 2008[9]. This model
quickly gained widespread acceptance for showing
how people interact with each other. The more
these five domains are equalized between parties,
the better the relationship. The key is to avoid
autocratic or hierarchical interactions and move
towards a more collaborative approach to improve
relationships.

In general, an autocratic leadership style typically
does not encourage or allow unity or self-
improvement. An autocratic class system is often
counterproductive, demoralizing, and ineffective,
and discourages collaboration. There may be times
when an autocratic approach is necessary, but if
collaboration is the goal, an autocratic approach will
stifle your initiatives. Those in authority have to be
willing to become a participant with less power in
order to promote a collaborative environment. It's
self-determination, and sharing ideas equally goes
a long way towards collaborative decision-making.
This is hard to do without practice and intent
because our natural tendency is to control and to
make our own decisions. Given our implicit biases,
this means we need to come to terms with them in
order to be proactive and promote understanding.
With patience, practice, and encouragement,
however, you can learn this technique and it can
help you promote collaborative decisions. When we
all feel valued and we are treated as equals, we are
more likely to share and participate.

Focus - Let's face it, as humans in today's hyperconnected world, we are easily distracted. We can fill our day with many activities and then wonder where the day went. When we focus on something and dedicate time to a task, it is possible to really apply energy to the activity, take constructive action, and deliver results. We need to focus not only on the task at hand, but focus can be broadened selectively to include systemic and interpersonal issues that have structured the environment in a particular way. As indicated above, this may involve minority points of view and attention to genuine equality of opportunity and engagement. Trust is built on such constructive actions, both at work and in personal relationships.

Typically focus should be on the underlying causes of an issue and the steps required to overcome barriers. Intellectual and emotional focus concentrates energy. Activities, interaction, stories, and fun are all ways to keep the energy level high. When focus is high, energy is high. This promotes mutual engagement. Having participants work on various activities together with team building techniques promotes collaboration. Distractions such as email can be a challenge, but we are learning new techniques to encourage interaction in virtual sessions[10]. For example, having an ice breaker at the beginning of a session is one way to encourage everyone to be on time for the virtual meeting and to set the stage, because they enjoy a break from the work routine. Another suggestion is sending participants the specific issue or idea on the agenda before the meeting; when this happens, they typically quickly focus on that activity individually and as a group. Having an agenda, topic, goal, and intent to focus goes a long way towards encouraging collaboration. Some questions to ask beforehand are:

- Why are we doing this?
- Who is accountable?
- How much time do we have?
- Is this a one-time meeting or part of a longer process?
- Who is taking meeting minutes?
- What is expected of participants?
- When are we meeting?
- Where are we meeting (is the space conducive to collaboration and are appropriate resources there)?
- What resources are being supplied (videos? YouTube? flip charts, markers, white board, post-it notes?)
- Who will do what by when as a result of this session? An action plan is needed.
- What is the final product expected to look like? Begin with the end in mind.

Begin with the end in mind. Is the final product a white paper, a power point presentation, an actual prototype, or something else?

Summary

So, there it is. We collaborate with others for a better result to maximize rewards and outcomes and tend to avoid pain. With the advent of artificial intelligence, soft skills are the critical skills of the future. Artificial intelligence is growing exponentially. Healthy competition is collaborative. It is rewarding on the bottom line, employee satisfaction, customer satisfaction and leadership development. By exploring your own and others' diversity you can enhance your understanding of yourself and others to connect better and develop better relationships. Encourage diverse thinking. Keep an open mind. Avoid hierarchies. Encourage those in authority to say for the purposes of this process, "I am just another team member," and then to play that role. Equality of ideas is key. Focus on the problem. Use techniques to raise the energy level. Be proactive and encouraging. Stay focused on the problem. Encourage fun, interaction, and participation, but also keep the end in mind. When these items are well thought out, you are far more likely to have an encouraging environment, and your chances for success using collaboration are significantly enhanced.

Chapter 2

FRAMING THE ISSUES FOR GROUPS

*"The strength of the team is each individual member.
The strength of each member is the team."*
—Phil Jackson

F rom the very beginning of any project, understand what your interests are and seek to understand the interest of other stakeholders. If you understand everyone's interests and address them, you can work towards a win-win solution. To provide a framework for this positive outcome, several elements need to be considered. The opposite happens when one person controls discussion and decision making, leaving no room for others to help work towards the common goal. But leaders who appreciate the way in which teamwork improves outcome, learn to rely on communication, collaboration, and understanding.

Consider People, Technology, and Information

When a leader wants to foster positive change there are three critical elements to consider: people, technology, and information. When looking for a win-win-with-others scenario, consider, address, and be proactive in all three areas.

In all communication[11] it is important to build trust between people by being straightforward, open, accepting, and responsible. This means operating and communicating with honesty and integrity. By being authentic and straightforward with others, it is possible to promote trust and understanding.

> By being authentic and straightforward with others, it is possible to promote trust and understanding.

Being open requires transparency. By communicating morally, ethically, and legally, you will encourage others to share their concerns with you. By encouraging questions from others, you demonstrate an accepting and free environment for exchange. Listening and responding with both facts and empathy are key components to building trust among team members. Open communication also requires avoidance of the two stinky twins of BO and BS—Blaming Others and Blaming Self. Stay above the line. It is important to accept that there will be alternative ways of thinking and even significant disagreements. But becoming angry, frustrated, or anxious loses focus on the problem.

It makes better sense that when personal tensions arise, the leader needs to be tough on the problem and soft on the people. All too often, our response to bad news or differing opinions is negative. This is natural. This quick and even hostile response to challenges has allowed us to survive as a species for a long time. However, most situations are not life-threatening. We need to calm the fire. We need to remain professional, responsible, and not overreact. We also need to take responsibility when working with others.

Being responsible means under promising and overdelivering. This demonstrates integrity. If a plumber tells you that the job will take a day and it only takes a half day you are very happy. If a plumber tells you that the job will take a day and it takes two days, you are not happy. Make it a practice to give yourself time for unexpected events and under-promise and overdeliver. By being responsible will promote trust.

The acronym I use for trust is SOAR. The acronym SOAR stands for being:

Straightforward
Open
Accepting
Responsible

When working with others, this acronym offers key advice. The commentary that follows explores this acronym in more detail.

Being straightforward means operating with clarity, integrity, and honesty. Honesty is oriented towards telling the truth. Integrity is based on moral principles, one of which is honesty, and following them religiously. You get right to the point. If you say you are going to do something by a given date, you should meet that date or come in earlier with the final product. If you can't make it, be honest and let the other party know the situation, explain what has happened, and provide the anticipated completion date. If your colleagues know they can count on you, this makes their planning easier as well.

Being open implies some degree of transparency. You not only ask for the task to be completed; you also explain why. If something is not going to work, you want to know, and you want to encourage them to speak up. You want them to share their concerns to make sure you don't overlook something.

Accepting others means to accept others from where they are coming from without prejudgments. Again, avoid BS and BO.

When you screw up admit it, apologize, and takes steps to make sure it won't happen again. The question is not what you or they can do, but rather what we can do together to make improvements going forward.

Be responsible for what happens. Have the backs of others. Walk the walk. Don't just talk the talk. The plumber example above brings this home. Under promise and overdeliver. If something goes wrong, bring it up right away, and then encourage teamwork to address the situation. After all we are in this together and we all have each other's backs.

Technology may be IT (hardware or software), mechanical devices, techniques, skills, methods, or processes. It has a broad definition. Technology is a two-edged sword. When it works correctly, is rolled out properly, and everyone is trained and adopts the new technology, it can provide huge benefits for a company. When it is not, it can be a disaster. The key is everyone must buy into the process and use the new technology.

The introduction of new technologies can be a source of friction and anxiety. A strong leader recognizes that simply imposing new devices, new software, or even new processes that involve unfamiliar instrumentation or intellectual infrastructure requires careful planning. The challenge is to have an efficient and effective implementation even though there are time constraints and other pressures. When things are rushed, the consequences can affect morale and material outcomes. For a technology implementation to go well, a ten-step, interest-based resolution process can help. An interest-based resolution means that the interests of the various parties have been presented and been listened to by you.

> An interest-based resolution means that the interests of the various parties have been presented and been listened to by you.

If the individuals affected have been heard, even though their ideas may not be fully implemented, they are more likely to buy into the new technologies. Let's take a look at what can be useful:

1. **Define** the situation, tackling only one issue at a time.
2. **Listen** in order to understand the facts and feelings that are expressed concerning the proposed technological changes. IT staff often are most interested in implementation of the new technology. But leaders need to be sure that there has been adequate preparation, including the testing of the systems so that new users are not responsible for working with faulty infrastructure. Other issues relate to users who may resent needing to learn a new technology or, indeed, even understanding it. A strong leader listens closely to understand initial anxiety, and then what problems seem to arise. If you don't have by in and a spirit of cooperation, you are setting yourself up for failure.
3. **Identify** and clarify interests around the technology, adopting the technology, implementing the technology, problems with the technology or anything else from adoption to implementation.
4. **Generate** options.
5. **Determine** the impacts of those options. Explore economic, social, and environmental impacts. Quantify and/or qualify them.
6. **Evaluate** the impacts of the options economically, socially, and environmentally. That is knowing what they are compare them between options. Explore how strong or weak the various options compare with each other economically, socially, and environmentally.
7. **Select** a solution, which may be one of the original options or a hybrid of the options presented if this is clear.
8. **Implement** the solution if this is clear or with what you now know consider returning to an earlier step.

9. **Test** the solution before implementing the solution. This can be a big issue. If possible, run the old and new systems at the same time until the new system can be tested, vented and accepted. If not, consider a localized test of the technology with a unit. Testing can save a lot of frustration, money and time.

10. **Consider BATNA and WATNTA,** if no solution can be found. This stands for the Best Alternative to a Negotiated Agreement (BATNA)[12] and the Worst Alternative to a Negotiated Agreement (WATNA)[13]. What BATNA means in a negotiation is that if you don't at least come to this level for an agreement, then you are prepared to walk away from the agreement. WATNA looks at what alternatives you have if you have to walk away. For example, you may have to hire someone else, reallocate resources, or take the project in another direction.

Following these steps will likely result in a positive change. Taking the time to manage the transition carefully when it comes to technology[14] can pay really big dividends later. If not, chances are the transition will manage you in terms of resources and time.

Sharing information[15] with your team starts with establishing a set of well-defined goals. Participants need to know and understand what is to be accomplished. They need to know who is responsible for accomplishing which tasks to achieve the goal, including communication of the tasks. Everyone should understand deadlines on when tasks must be accomplished and in what order. One good strategy for the leader and the team is to be sure that all participants know the goal and feel that they have full information. Asking for consensus on where

> One good strategy for the leader and the team is to be sure that all participants know the goal and feel that they have full information.

everyone is currently at is important at the end of every meeting to ensure team understanding and good communications.

Given that information is essential, and that clarity also requires some level of agreement, the leader needs to assess the group. Often this requires additional dialogue. It may turn out that not everyone was in agreement with who was doing what by when. Ensuring it is clear who will do what by when before leaving any session will go a long way toward understanding the project's information and communication needs and strategies. The answers will define who is responsible for obtaining and providing information in a timely manner to key stakeholders.

Additionally, consider the risks associated with all information that needs to be shared. What is the likelihood of problems arising and how might those problems be handled proactively? Providing information without clarification can cause misunderstandings. Others may not know what is expected of them once they have the information. Still others may have thought they were supposed to do something or take actions without understanding the implications. Use the same ten-step process above to define your approach. For this reason, be ready to supply both before-and-after information. Knowing there can be misunderstanding when communicating information, consider both pre- and post-implementation support.

Not everyone receives or digests information in the same way. Be prepared to review, revise, and test the information processes you implement. Expect the unexpected to take place. What can be learned by unexpected outcomes and how can they be addressed? Remember to keep key stakeholders in the loop and address all three areas: people, technology, and information.

Model Integrity During Transitions

Keep in mind that leading change during difficult times can be particularly trying. Have you ever seen a leader try to implement change under very trying circumstances? I did in the 1980's, when I was with the U.S. Army Corps of Engineers. One day, our entire district was called together for an impromptu meeting. An announcement was made that in one year our employee count in this district would be reduced from 264 to 128. You could have heard a pin drop. You could hear and feel the collective concern. Would I lose my job? Would I no longer be working with these people who had become my dear friends? What would happen after the layoffs? Facing our questions and fears head on, our Colonel demonstrated all the characteristics of a true leader. He told us he would share whatever information he could legally. He told us he wanted to help each one of us land on our feet. He was completely authentic.

The Colonel understood how to be honest and operate with integrity. He didn't lie and he didn't sugarcoat anything. He cared and we knew he cared. We trusted him. He sought advice from Human Resources (HR) up the chain of command and from other sources. He met with employees to hear and address their concerns. In return, he trusted us to continue to do our best, even though we might be laid off soon. He not only said he would help us, he actually helped us. He had dedicated HR employees that reached out to each individual one on one to help each person through the process. Many employees stayed with the organization and were moved by the organization to job postings in other locations. Some were able to take early retirement with full benefits. There were others not yet retirement eligible by a year or two that would like to have retired if they could. The Colonel went to the Under Secretary of the Army and asked to make specific exceptions to give them the equivalent age or time in service to be able to retire early. Some were helped with new job searches, resumes and other assistance. The organization really went the extra mile for everyone. The Colonel set the tone and made sure all support people were on board to go the extra mile. I am not aware of anyone that felt the organization didn't do everything it could and truly demonstrated a caring concern for each employee. This was a tribute to great leadership and follow up by that leader.

Remember, "It's not about me. It's all about we. But we starts with me." The Colonel recognized a difficult conversation, he needed to come at it with a positive attitude and a genuine desire to help. You have to focus on understanding others' concerns and apprehensions. Ask questions:

- Can you tell me more about your concerns?
- Why do you feel that way?
- What information can I give you?
- What would you like to have happen?
- What concerns or worries do you have?
- What would it take for you to feel satisfied?
- What can I do to help you?
- What have we not covered that you would like me to know?
- Are there any other concerns or problems?

Although your conversation has an agenda, listen actively to the group. Fully understanding their concerns is critical to mapping out the transition processes that they will follow. Transitions are generally gradual. They involve gains and losses. A good transition is at best a two-steps-forward-and-only-one-step-back process. During more difficult stages of a transition, it is expected that there will be more steps backward than forward. Unknowns and surprises are also likely to cause setbacks. Unexpected technical, administrative, or managerial concerns can arise. It would be nice if such surprises could be mapped out with a neat set of responses, but that's just not how it works. The unexpected is always challenging to measure in terms of seriousness, urgency, or importance. For these reasons, transitions require constant attention to the impacts they are having on individuals. One person can easily move on while another person may feel deeply hurt, left out, and grieving. These feelings are real. Expect a host of feelings to emerge at various times with transitions. Being as prepared as possible while remaining flexible to address the unexpected leads to a winning situation for all stakeholders.

If you want to bring about change, you must model it. Involve your team and collaborate on joint interests. Help others break out of the past. If you want to lead your team successfully through a difficult transition, you must push through your own concerns and fears for the sake of others. That's what leaders do. As a leader, you must remain focused and be there for your people. Create a supportive environment that allows everyone time to transition. Even if you may be negatively impacted by the coming change, you must remain positive for others. Your positive attitude and appropriate enthusiasm set the stage for how others will react.

Manage the Change Process with Your Team

The three phases associated with change are endings, the neutral time, and new beginnings. These three phases are fluid and require constant attention. The three phases are also uniquely experienced by each individual.

When people in an organization realize change is coming, not everyone will anticipate that an **ending** is something that needs to be addressed. Loss of a vested interest, emotional support, financial stability, or some life experience that holds value may have a profound negative impact on individuals or an entire group. In these times, a leader can help others understand that indeed they must understand they need to

- Let things go
- Understand that old realities are gone

- Accept that old identities are lost
- Grasp that old connections are changing
- Deal with loss

When this happens there may very well be grief. A key to caring is to listen with empathy. Allowing people to grieve gives them permission to move on. The following are examples of what might be lost:

- Money
- Financial stability
- Security
- Turf
- Status
- Power
- Influence
- Relationships
- Future dreams
- Meaningful work
- Control
- Personal identity
- Friendships

As a leader you need to acknowledge the loss. Own it as a leader. Have an open discussion with those impacted. Understand and acknowledge people's feelings and be sensitive to the needs of individuals. Grief is real and natural when loss occurs.

Even as you grieve, help yourself and others by celebrating the legacy of what has been achieved. Think of it like celebrating someone's life at a funeral. Consider having a potluck, a party, or sort of a wake to acknowledge how well things worked before. Pay tribute to the past. Consider the organization's accomplishments. Remember the trials, tribulations, funny stories, and successes. This type of celebration can bring the first stage of closure and prepare a path for everyone to move from an ending to the next stage, the neutral time.

As people leave the ending phase there is less grieving. The **neutral time** is a time of transition. During this phase, there is uncertainty at every level. Although things are gone, rules and circumstances may be in a state of flux. Expectations are continually changing. The roles of participants are up in the air. Titles, positions, and who has power are all in a state of flux.

There are positives and negatives during this transition. For many this will seem chaotic. The neutral time can and be very frustrating and aggravating. On the plus side, the neutral time phase can become a time of tremendous creativity. It provides an opportunity to drop the old rules and systems and create fresh and better systems and processes.

Own your emotions and reactions. As a leader in the neutral time, you'll need to realize that you are human and have feelings just like everybody else. Be honest with others, too, and work to remain authentic, realistic, and pragmatic while staying focused on the big picture.

Ask yourself key questions:

- How will I benefit or not benefit from this change?
- How will the organization benefit? Or not?
- How will others benefit? Or not?

Recognize how your answers might influence your leadership during a big transition. There is a fair amount of ambiguity and thus uncertainty during such transitions. Particularly as a leader, you must let go of old rules, expectations, and roles.

Remember that you and your team are in this together. Be there for each other. Support one another. Eventually, this leads to new beginnings.

During the **new beginnings** phase, you must decide how you will act. You might still be managing your own losses. Come to grips with this and address your own feelings. Remember to take care of yourself physically, mentally, and spiritually too. Your style of communication during this phase is critical. If you are positive, others will feed off your energy. If you are negative, others will be dragged down with you. Determine how you will act as a leader as you start this new phase. Leaders complain up. They don't complain laterally or down the chain of command.

During these times, you need to be open to understanding things in new ways. Accept new values, attitudes, and identities that will set you and your team up for success. The results could be higher productivity, customer satisfaction, and employee engagement. As a change leader, put everything up for consideration—every process, service or product should be on trial for its life. It may be necessary to abandon processes, services, or products of minimal value even if a few good years remain. As a change leader, this means that you will need to establish and promote new processes, services, or products that are even better. Think of examples from your own experiences with technology, processes, evaluation systems, production standards, and other important elements.

Resistance to change is to be expected. Involve employees in the transition planning. Consider including some of the naysayers. If they buy in, others are more likely to follow. If the naysayers really understand the process, and are part of it, they might become some of your most active supporters. Encourage employees to share personal concerns. What are their fears and apprehensions? Put everything on the table—concerns, fears, unhappiness, stubbornness. These emotions are all real and worthy of acknowledgement. And, therein, lies an opportunity. If someone fears excessive work pressure, address their concern. If costs are perceived to be too high, consider various options. It may be necessary to face the fact that various stakeholders don't believe the rewards are adequate to adopt the change. Questions need to be addressed if you wish to be successful.

Encourage clear, honest communication, and learn from it. Along the way, be clear about the purpose of the change, which may have been forgotten along the way. Remind everyone of the new system's intentions and potential benefits. Folks can get bogged down in the details of the transition and lose the vision. It's your job as a change leader to make sure that doesn't happen. Throughout the process build trust and respect between you, your group, and the change initiator. It takes a lot of hard work, blood, sweat and tears to get to a new beginning. Don't forget to celebrate this achievement.

Summary

This chapter provides a framework to help your people experience success during transition. It is important that you address people issues, changes in technology (the 10-step process), and information sharing. As a leader you need to transition with the change, adapt to the complexities, and model an appropriate response. This can be particularly difficult when it doesn't feel good to you, but as a leader you need be there for your team as a positive influence. Realize that there are endings, a neutral time, and new beginnings. These are fluid. Endings implies both grief and a celebration of past accomplishments. Neutral times are both chaotic and creative in nature. New beginnings offer opportunities and challenges. Be a positive force to help yourself and your team moving forward.

Chapter 3

ALIGNING SOCIAL SKILLS WITH DIFFICULT PEOPLE

"The secret to success is good leadership, and good leadership is all about making the lives of your team members or workers better."
—Tony Dungy

Nobody gets along with everybody. This chapter addresses how to align your skills with those of others who you may find difficult to work with. Sometimes the different perspective is evident, but other times it is complicated to identify why we don't get along. When that is the case, working together can be very challenging. This chapter looks specifically at skills to help overcome negative emotional reactions by applying specific strategies. The following chapter will help you to manage conflict at work with people you and others find difficult.

We have all had to work with difficult people in our careers. They may be a supervisor, peer, subordinate, vendor, customer, or stakeholder. Whatever their name or title, this person just irks you. For some reason you just can't seem to get along with this person. What can be done? As hard as it might seem, you need to approach the person with an open mind and an intention to really understand what they may be thinking. You must center yourself and calm the fire within. You need to work with the person in a civil manner, and that may require that you understand their needs and interests.

Overcoming Negative Emotional Reactions at Work

The first step is to ask yourself why you view the other party as difficult. What is it about them or their actions that gives you pause? Label your thoughts and write them down. Then, explore the reasons why these characteristics or behaviors trigger you.

After you have identified the attributes or behaviors that are irritating, ask the question of yourself or your team: Could I or we actually be encouraging their behavior by what I (we) am (are) doing? Could I be part of the problem? What are my own feelings about the situation we share? Sometimes we react negatively to others and we don't know why. Could it be because we have similar faults? Psychologists say this can contribute to our irritation.

Maybe you have someone on your team who is toxic. This person is actually undermining your team's ability to work together. How do you handle this? Start with considering their motivations. Are there personal issues or incentives that inadvertently lead them to behave negatively? Is it possible this person has ownership of an issue and only sees one side of the problem? Is it possible this person is not interested in or capable of exploring the interests of others? Do they prefer litigation to negotiation? As you assess the situation, consider the perspectives of all your team members. If others agree with you that this person is difficult to work with, consider exploring your own biases and those of your team members. Sometimes these biases can negatively impact conversations and negotiations. If you mutually agree this person is difficult to work with, then it may be worth a conversation with your team members to see what we can do to try and turn this situation around. If you maintain an open atmosphere with an intention to help you may be able to discover ways you can try to overcome your situation.

At some time in your career, you are likely to find yourself in a high-pressure situation with someone you don't know personally and whose demeanor is disconcerting. Such an encounter doesn't have to end badly, but it does present challenges. Stay calm. Listen actively and try to understand the other party's interests before pursuing your own. We all like to be listened to. So, ask questions. Hear the other person's concerns before communicating your own.

> We all like to be listened to. So, ask questions. Hear the other person's concerns before communicating your own.

We are all familiar with feedback. At its best, feedback is constructive criticism to improve how something was done in the past. Consider an alternative: feedforward.[16] With feedforward, the situation is addressed by exploring what would be done differently in the future, perhaps with collaboration. Instead of focusing on the past the two key words are "we" and "future". We are in this together. How could we work together to come up with a better approach for next time? With feedforward, employees and managers work together to implement positive process change for the future without undue commentary. Similarly, in a negotiation, two or more parties work together to find a solution that meets their requirements and interests. With feedforward in a negotiation, those involved must work together to address concerns focusing on the future.

Another useful technique is the NIP model. NIP stands for Notice, Investigate, Problem solve.

- **N**otice Feelings
- **I**nvestigate further
- **P**roblem solve together

Interpersonal skills need to be brought into play even as problems are defined and then addressed; if someone's facial expressions, body language, tone of voice and/or verbiage indicates differences of opinion, further inquiry might be warranted. For example, the discussion leader might ask: "It appears to me that you might not be fully on board with this plan yet. Do you have concerns before we move on?" If the person does have concerns, follow up with additional questions or statements, such as, "Please, tell me more..." or "Why is that?" or "What do you think made you feel this way?" This technique can be applied at work, at home, or in nearly any setting. After you have noticed feelings and investigated further it may be possible to work together to define the problem properly. Take care not to define the problem too narrowly or broadly. Pause and make sure you are focusing on the right problem and not the personalities of the people involved with the problem. Our first inclination is often to blame others. Individuals may be responsible, but this should not be the focus. Define the problem so that you can explore it together without placing blame. Explore what the positives may be if the problem was reworded in such a way as to overcome the situation.

I was working with a team of technical people as the team lead. Each of the team members was highly capable and knew their area well. Two of the team members were not from our team, but had insights from the client's perspective that would be very helpful to the entire team. As we discussed the project and what direction we might take with the project, my team members had very definite opinions. The two outsiders raised good issues that were well received overall by my team. However, one of my team members started to become fairly entrenched with respect to a particular issue. Her commentary tended to cut off one of the outside members' comments or belittle her. There seemed to be some tension in the room. We took a break.

I spoke to my team member, and she shared what she did not like about some of the comments of the outside team member. I spoke to the outside team member to see how she was feeling and what she thought of the commentary from my team member. It turns out they both had additional insights, but neither had gone into detail with respect to their reasoning. Each was hoping the other would simply concede. After the break I asked additional questions of each of them to identify additional concerns and to elaborate on their earlier comments. Once they went into greater detail each gained additional credibility with each other and the group. Once everyone understood the underlying concerns, it was fairly straightforward to come up with an appropriate alternative and decision. The statement of "please tell me more" and the questions of "Why is that?" and "Why do you feel that way?" helped bring out additional information to shed light on the problem at hand. Prior to the break the two viewed each other negatively. At the end of the session, both thought the other party was reasonable and had some good ideas. Don't underestimate the power of these simple questions.

Consider this scenario: an employee forgot a critical deadline. The client is upset. While investigating the situation, the employee apologizes and explains that they simply forgot the deadline. It was a mistake, a simple oversight. Rather than blaming the employee, explore what could be done mutually to prevent the oversight from happening again in the future. Brainstorm ideas together regarding scheduling, calendar issues, developing a drop file with interim completion dates, or other approaches. By tackling the problem together, you create a positive team-building experience out of a problem. By asking open ended questions[17], actively listening[18] and working together you have an opportunity to build trust[19]. If you approach issues and concerns in this manner, you might be surprised by what you can accomplish with your team.

Be Prepared, Practice, and Perform

You know how it is. You know what you are supposed to do. You are supposed to listen. This was introduced with The Collaboration Effect and will be elaborated on in Chapter 6. You are supposed to be empathetic and develop a relationship. That is great in theory, but when you are engaged with a difficult person, that is not easy. All you want to do is share what you have on your mind. How can you learn to close your mouth and listen? It is logically easy enough to know you really should listen, but emotionally can you control yourself and learn to listen?

In my book *Peaceful Resolutions*[20], I devote an entire chapter to the concept of de-escalation. There I provide a more in-depth discussion of these topics. There is also a chapter on listening. That book provides a more in-depth commentary for your consideration. In this book, the focus is different. It's about having discussions with difficult people. You need to control your own temper—your primal animal instincts—and listen carefully. You know this is what you *should* do, but you're not sure that you can pull it off. So, how do you train yourself? First of all, you tell yourself what really matters[21].

> **Prepare** - You need to calm yourself before you begin any crucial conversation with a difficult person. Rather than writing down what you want to say, list what you believe the other party wants to say. This will help you to be more empathic and to listen with an open mind.

> Society teaches us how to argue, debate and confront in the face of conflict. However, if the goal is to improve our relationship and work together more collaboratively in the future, listening is key. Try to determine if there are multiple issues, what they are, how strongly the other side feels about

the various issues, and their interest level on each issue. Prepare a thorough list of what you believe to be the other side's interests. Then, convert the list to open-ended questions that you can ask. If you want to start a rich conversation, ask open-ended questions[22] to encourage open-ended answers. That is, ask questions that will require more than yes or no answers.

Practice - Practice makes perfect. If active listening, remaining calm and empathy are not your strengths, then practice these skills. Practice will improve your performance in tough situations. Try and build an empathetic relationship. See if you can concisely summarize the key points even better than the other person. Focus on the problem, not the personality across the table. Remain respectful and empathetic toward the other person no matter how difficult the task. Ask your open-ended questions in a calm, slow, and reassuring voice. Refer to notes, if necessary. Paraphrase what you hear and summarize them. Share what you have heard in a concise manner to demonstrate to the other party that you are really listening. Take notes. Ask open-ended follow-up questions, drilling deeper into the issue. This demonstrates genuine attention and concern and your intention to try to build a bridge, an emotional relationship, despite your differences.

Perform - Role play can help you reinforce what you have learned in the first two steps. Reach out to someone you know and trust and work with them on a less challenging issue. Practice for the discussion that is ahead with the difficult person. Use the techniques you have learned in the first two steps in this less difficult situation. After the exercise, review with your practice partner what worked and did not work.

Review with your practice partner what worked and did not work.

Give yourself feedforward on what you will do when dealing with the difficult situation that awaits you. Summarize what you believe the other party's perspective is and ask, "Do I understand your perspective?" If the answer is yes, then you have captured the idea and confirmed that you indeed do understand. If not, ask more open-ended questions until the answer is yes. Learning these skills is a process. Remember, your goal is to understand the other person's perspective. Keep asking questions until there is nothing left for you to learn. As with any activity repeating the performance will continue to enhance your abilities. Give yourself a break and celebrate small wins. Pat yourself on the back and keep learning from your practice experiences.

Try Self-Distancing

Studies show that speaking to yourself in the second or third person rather than the first person can change your emotional focus. You may ask why does this matter. When you find yourself starting to feel angry, this self-distracting technique can and will help you better regulate your emotions. This is a very powerful tool. The thing is, you must remember to do it. Here are two steps to help you control your temper and become known as the person that remains cool under pressure.

Have you ever heard a professional athlete speaking about him or herself in the third person during an interview? For example, LeBron James may say to a reporter, "LeBron James did not have his best game today." Did you ever ask why someone of LeBron James's stature might do this? It's because they have been taught to use self-distancing. If we think of ourselves outside of ourselves, we have a very different and often more positive perspective to study the situation and remain calm. It is called self-distancing. You can practice this to help you look at yourself in a more neutral light. Try it and see if it might help you, too.

Speak to yourself. For example, when someone cuts you off in traffic by using your own name. In this situation, I might say, "Whoa! That was close, Mike. Who knows where he is going or why, but thank goodness he is past me." The third person focus can help you calm yourself. Whether you are a professional athlete talking about yourself to reporters, or addressing a stressful situation, neuroscience clearly indicates that self-distancing has a calming effect[23]. Consider following up with something like, "Mike, I wonder what is going on in that guy's world?" Let's take this technique a step further. Ask yourself questions and shift the reference from, "Why do I feel this way?" to "Why does (my name) feel this way?" This simple shift can change the way you perceive the issue.

> Ask yourself questions and shift the reference from, "Why do I feel this way?" to "Why does (my name) feel this way?" This simple shift can change the way you perceive the issue.

It is not easy to shift into this third-party perspective. Neuroscientists do not know why making this shift can have a profound impact[24], but the fact is research shows that it can.[25]

In the heat of the moment, it takes real effort to shift focus. Our natural tendency is to fight back and defend ourselves. However, if you are conscious of this inclination and make the effort, you can use this simple technique to remain calm and discuss the problem at hand without negative emotions.

The other party may actually be trying to move you in a negative direction, hoping you will make a mistake or become angry and say something that can be used against you. The other party may just want to be antagonistic because they are frustrated. Either way, you lose the upper hand, if they push your buttons and you react negatively.

If you can keep your cool while the other party is losing theirs, you are likely to be successful with the situation you are trying to accomplish. Remaining calm is in itself is a win. By remaining cool, firm, professional and collected this can change the entire temperament of the situation. This will change how you are perceived by the other party and by those observing you in the situation.[26] Others will perceive you as a cool character under pressure. You can be trusted as that person others count on to be neutral and consistent in tough situations.

As stated earlier, this takes practice. Consider this as a starting point: Write yourself a little note that says, "Why do I feel this way? Why does (your name) feel this way?" and place it in your pocket. When you find yourself becoming angry with someone else, reach into your pocket and touch the piece of paper. It will remind you to use the third-person technique, which can go a long way towards de-escalating[27] almost any situation. Imagine yourself as cool under pressure. Wouldn't it be nice to be perceived as the person who does not overreact to others' negativity? Such a reputation might even help your career. As a last resort if nothing else works, do your best to avoid the other person. If the other party does not want to interact with you, simply move on. Don't take it personally.

Summary

In this chapter we have covered ways for you to overcome emotional reactions and conflicts at work. Now you can apply feedforward as a positive technique that demonstrates how "we can work together" to take appropriate actions next time rather than providing feedback. In the future you will focus on being tough on the problem and soft on the people. Before entering into a potential tense situation, you have learned how to prepare, practice, and perform better in the future. Having learned about self-distancing you can try this technique to shift your thinking by asking yourself questions. All of these practices can help you align your skills when dealing with change going forward.

Chapter 4

INTRODUCTION TO THE COLLABORATION EFFECT

*"It is amazing how much people can get done if they
do not worry about who gets the credit."*
—Sandra Swinney

C onflict is not always a bad thing. Without some element of conflict or stress that alerts us to danger, we might not have survived as a species [28]. Even Tibetan Monks need an element of stress to keep their hearts beating. We all need a certain amount of stress to be alive. Conflict indicates that someone cares. If no one cared, there would be no conflict. As such, conflict is not inherently bad and can even be good. When two parties have a conflict, they unconsciously determine what they see as the facts. Considering their perception of the facts they identify issues. Emotions can be triggered positively or negatively depending on the perception of the issues. These emotions may give rise to interests that can help them develop their positions. Often it is possible to recognize initial positions. However, it is only with further questioning and analysis that it is possible to uncover other's deeper interests to work towards a resolution. While you have met some of the following ideas in earlier chapters, here there will be a focus on working into successful collaboration.

Behind every position there is at least one interest, and that interest holds the seed to a solution. Positions are the demands each party has and what they will or not do to meet those demands. Positions tend to polarize. Many times, these positions are obvious to the individual and to the other party. Other times, the positions of the opposing parties may not be as obvious and require further explo-

> Behind every position there is at least one interest, and that interest holds the seed to a solution.

ration. As the parties dig deeper by asking open-ended questions, it is often possible to uncover hidden interests that may lead to a mutually acceptable solution. Instead of the golden rule (treat others as you would like to be treated), try applying the platinum rule: treat others as *they* would like to be treated. When working with cross cultural, generational, or other differences where misunderstandings can easily develop, the application of the platinum rule can be extremely helpful.

Developing Your Skills

On its surface, The Collaboration Effect is really quite simple. In order to build bridges with another party towards a common purpose or closure it is necessary to develop connecting relationships,[29] listen actively,[30] and educate judiciously.[31] When these elements have been accomplished, it is far more likely you will be able to negotiate closure[32]. Let's briefly explore each of the three elements associated with The Collaboration Effect.

First, connecting with someone else requires building an understanding of them, their background, their values, and their interests.

If you know the other person well, you may have such insights. If you know nothing or little about a person, it may be necessary to do some research. Consider using social media and learning what you can from Facebook, LinkedIn, Instagram, Twitter, Reddit, Pinterest, and other social media. Network with others that you know. What insights do they have with respect to the other party?

Look for and discover common interests, so that you can bring them up in a face-to-face or virtual meeting. This may enable you to have conversations beyond the topic of conflict. Shared educational institutions, a common hobby or history, veteran status, children, pets, travel—all are ice breakers that can open conversations and, if necessary, ease tensions. The key is to discover an area of a shared emotional connection. Keep this in mind from the outset of your conversations, and look for openings.

Second, listening actively means making a real effort to understand the other party logically and emotionally. Often in a conflict, we're on edge. We ready ourselves to refute the other party's commentary rather than really listening to them. This is what formal debate is all about. In everyday life, we need to turn this model on its head because successful conflict resolution requires collaboration, which in turn requires active listening.

Listening in the middle of a conflict is hard. It takes a concerted effort and it takes practice to keep quiet and really listen. It requires putting 100 percent of your energy into the act of listening. This requires your mind, words, tone, facial expressions, and body language to be completely focused on listening. To actively listen you need to paraphrase, summarize, ask open ended questions and empathize.

Third, educate judiciously after thoroughly listening to the other party. Education is best when it incorporates subtle understandings. Don't use words like always and never. Educating judiciously is purposeful, has an end in mind, and requires anticipating how the other party prefers to learn. Don't sell. Rather be helpful and address anticipated questions and concerns. You want to be conclusive, but not in a demanding way. Work with the other party to promote understanding. Your attitude must be helpful. Make the other person the hero. Give them the golden bridge to retreat honorably if needed. If you have expertise, demonstrate it humbly. Do not be a know-it-all. If you are an expert on a topic, consider asking questions that lead the other party towards an understanding of the situation from your perspective.

> In order to build bridges with another party towards a common purpose or closure it is necessary to develop connecting relationships, listen actively, and educate judiciously.

By connecting relationships, listening actively, and educating judiciously you can apply The Collaboration Effect to build bridges to a common purpose and lead to negotiating closure. The Collaboration Effect is based on neuroscience. The neuroscience elements incorporated into The Collaboration Effect are connecting[33] relationships, listening actively[34] and educating[35] judiciously. It doesn't just happen. Rather it takes practice and due diligence to master.

Build Trust

Much has been written about trust and why it is important[36]. If you don't have the trust of the people sitting across the table from you, then you are in real trouble if you are trying to collaborate with them. Trust is teamed up with The Collaboration Effect[37]. In the last endnote commentary, there is a deeper dive into trust and trustworthiness, with two of the three elements of The Collaboration Effect (connecting relationships and listening actively).

Trust is "a firm belief in reliability, truth, ability, or strength in someone or something." I am going to focus on the "someone" here.

In that sense, trust means you have confidence in someone. You believe they are reliable. You can count on them.

Have you ever noticed how much other children, your children or your grandchildren trust you? How much faith they have in you? What they are willing to do with and for you? My wife and I were at a playground at the local park with my two granddaughters, ages 2 and 4. We were with some other kids, and everyone was having fun. There was a three-sided climbing wall that rose up about 12 feet with a center flat section about 8 inches in diameter. I had encouraged each of the girls to climb the wall. Of course, I was in position and I would be ready to catch or assist them if they should become concerned or fall. I encouraged the older granddaughter. She climbed up about three-quarters of the way and then climbed down. The younger granddaughter climbed up a few feet and then she came back down.

We kept playing with a host of climbable items around the park. Then to my surprise my two-year-old granddaughter went back to the climbing wall and with no fear at all climbed all the way up to the top of the wall. I ran over and quickly climbed up behind her just as she reached the top. I watched her sit confidently on a small platform atop the wall. I smiled, but of course, inside I was very nervous in case she might fall. "Papa," she said calmly. "I heard you say to my sister that she could do it, and I thought I can, too." I congratulated her on her accomplishment and then I suggested we climb back down together—with me acting as a safety net should she slip. That's what complete trust looks like. I told my granddaughter and her sister that I had confidence in them and not to be afraid. "Try something new," I said...and that's just what that trusting little two-year-old did. The Collaboration Effect is all about trust.

Trust is the key for every leader. This is as at the very core of developing leadership. General Colin Powell offers great advice in a less than 3-minute video. Good leaders are trusted by followers. They take them to the next level. The essence of the video is that you know when you have trust when your people follow you because they are curious. Why? Because you built up that trust through selfless service. You serve selflessly. You prepare them. When you are tired, cold, hungry, and scared, you don't show that you are tired, cold, hungry or scared. Acknowledge the challenges but face them with confidence—Powell thus survived many tight situations.

As a new front-line manager, I took training on leadership and developed a leadership mantra that worked for me. It served me as a front-line manager, middle manager and at the executive level. I am offering this to you to help you with your leadership development.

- Thank your employees once a week for something specific.
- Get them the resources they need from their perspective and don't micromanage.
- Give them a chance to shine in achievement and leadership.

That's it. It is that easy. However, focus and consistency are key. On the first point I worked with my first group that expanded from 9 technical experts in one location to 21 technical experts and two support staff in three different metropolitan areas. How could I possibly thank 23 people once a week for something specific? I couldn't. I had built a culture over time to have employees do this with one another and keep me informed so I could piggyback on their initiatives. On the second point, don't send your employees to carry out a task without the right resources. If you do you are setting them up for failure. That will destroy trust. On the third point, give them a chance to shine at work and even outside of work to support them with their passion. If you do these three things consistently and with all of your employees equitably you will build trust. They will see that you care, you are consistent, you are equitable, and you include everyone with this process.

Trust and the development of trust is presented in additional sources[38]. In order to build trust, you have to get to know your employees. The more you know about them, the easier it is to build trust. You have to make the effort. Understand them and their interests outside of work too. Let them know that you care and show it with the questions you ask and the interest you have in them. This is even harder with remote employees, so you have to make an extra effort with them. You need to find ways to bring your employees together. Be creative. Ask them for their ideas on what they want to do. Fostering trust is a key leadership behavior.

Others have to be confident in you. They have to have faith in you. They have to know they can count on you. You have to be committed to them. Being consistent day in and day out is the key. Encourage others to interact with you and other members of your team. Mean what you say. Say what you mean. Establish positive trust enhancing group norms.

Nothing destroys trust more than your violating a private or professional confidence. Being unreliable and not doing what you say also undermines trust. When you lose trust, self-preservation and self-interest take over. People become more guarded with their actions. You lose the ability to lead a team. Productivity decreases. The flow of information is slower. Goals are not met. People become far more calculating in the way they interact with others. They withhold information. Deception and lack of truth begin to flourish. Maybe ninety percent of relevant information is provided, but not everything that is needed. This can set you and other team members up for failure.

While it may be expedient to move quickly and not disclose what may or may not be essential information, often transparency can save time and resources going forward., Once trust has been lost, negotiations can bog down as the level of verification can grow exponentially, causing a significant increase in time resources and potential delays.

From neuroscience it has been found that as trust is enhanced with others through neurotransmitter oxytocin[39]. Oxytocin is referred to as the "cuddle hormone" because it is released when people cuddle or bond socially[40]. This is directly related to building and managing relationships. Many underestimate the value of building a relationship, listening closely, and educating the other side in a negotiation. Often these three elements take up to seventy five percent of the time of a successful, complex negotiation.

For these reasons trust is very important. Trust really is critical with your team and when you interact with others. You need to continually keep confidences with others. Build trust. Maintain trust. The downside risk to not having trust is very significant. Trying to bring back or build trust once trust is broken is an uphill battle. Don't jeopardize trust. Continually work to reinforce trust by consistency in your own behavior. Now that we understand trust, how important it is, and what happens when you lose trust what about being trustworthy?

Trustworthy, Trust Collaboration

Trustworthy means we are deserving of trust. We are thought of as being reliable and dependable. When we are trustworthy, others say that we deserve their trust. Trustworthy individuals have several common traits:

- They are authentic. They know who they are.
- They are compassionate, consistent, and considerate. They seek to genuinely understand the feelings of others. They are friendly, generous, and polite. They are also reliably kind, helpful, and caring.
- They have integrity and are resourceful. They are honest and have a strong moral compass. They are quick to adopt and use resources in clever ways.

How do trust and trustworthiness tie into The Collaboration Effect?

The Collaboration Effect is all about developing trust with another party. The two building blocks of trust are developing connecting relationships and listening actively. The Collaboration Effect won't work without trust. Trust is a subset of The Collaboration Effect.

Often when trust is lost, such as in a personal relationship, it is nearly impossible for the parties to collaborate on something going forward. It is very hard to re-establish trust once it has been lost or broken. When starting from a negative relationship it is very hard to de-escalate the situation to a neutral position in order to begin to build trust for collaboration going forward. It starts with an apology[41] , but then there must also be a commitment to change. The proof is in your actions. If we apologize and then we continue the behavior, it is impossible to build trust.

Summary

This chapter introduced you to the building blocks of The Collaboration Effect. These are building connecting relationships to engage with others; listening actively to really understand where the other person is coming from and why; and educating judiciously by explaining where you are coming from and why to promote a better understanding. Two of the elements of The Collaboration Effect tie directly into building trust, namely connecting relationships and listening actively. Building trust is essential. The example with my granddaughter demonstrated what implicit trust is like. When we build trust with others, we are perceived as being trustworthy. When we are perceived as being trustworthy, others take our integrity and honesty for granted, and that allows us to engage and collaborate with each other.

Chapter 5

CONNECTING RELATIONSHIPS

*"Whatever affects one directly, affects all indirectly. I can
never be what I ought to be until you are what you ought
to be. This is the interrelated structure of reality."*
— *Rev. Dr. Martin Luther King, Jr.*

As discussed in Chapter 4, The Collaboration Effect has three elements: developing connecting relationships, listening actively, and educating judiciously in order to collaborate with opposing parties and reach a negotiated closure. These three elements are naturally intertwined and needed to achieve a successful negotiation. The focus of this chapter is on developing connecting relationships. Focusing on developing relationships from the beginning can pay big dividends long term. As you consider closure from the beginning keep in mind eventual negotiations. As negotiations are underway, participants necessarily step back and evaluate how much effort may be necessary for each element, developing a plan and adapting the plan as the negotiation proceeds.

Life is full of conflicts and collaboration with a goal of achieving some result. This is true at both work and home. It's a part of every aspect of our lives. That's where real connecting relationships come in. But how do we develop connecting relationships? It is about understanding where other people are coming from and respecting their underlying interests. Consider validating others by focusing on being interested, not on being interesting, in order to develop an engaging relationship.

> Consider validating others by focusing on being interested not on being interesting in order to develop an engaging relationship.

Have you ever been on a sports team, part of group, or on a special group assignment where you really worked well together? How did that feel? Everyone had everyone else's back. Everyone looked out for one another. You shared a common goal. You didn't care who got the credit, if you achieved the goal; it was all about reaching it together. You shared things with each other you didn't necessarily share with others. It was a memorable experience for all the right reasons. Sometimes you really connect with a member of the team in such a situation.

I want to share a short story about one such team. Six of us were brought to headquarters to help realign the finance and accounting function for a $10.5 billion dollar entity. My office was in the Twin Cities area. The project required working in Washington, D.C., and coming home every other weekend for five months. I was the only person from Minnesota. The rest of the team was from the D.C. area. I am a white Anglo-Saxon Protestant. Another member of the team was a Black woman from Washington D.C. We were both married and we both had children. She invited me to go with her family to watch her son play in a basketball tournament. I jumped at the chance. It was in Prince George's County, one of the very successful majority African American Counties in the country. The gym was packed, and I realized I was the only Caucasian there.

This gave me an uncomfortable feeling, but I never felt threatened or ill at ease. I had grown up in an area with some Blacks, Chicanos, and Asians, but in a predominately white neighborhood. However, this was the first time I was literally the only white person in a crowded gymnasium with plenty of bleacher seating on both sides. It just felt odd to be a minority. I watched the game and I had a lot of fun. I cheered for her son with the rest of her family.

The next day at work I thanked her for inviting me to the game to see her son play, allowing me to meet her family, and for the overall experience. Having for the first time felt what it was like to be the only white person in a group, this gave me a much greater insight and a glimpse into what she must have to go through every day. I honestly had never really given it much thought before. It made me far more self-aware. Her initiative brought me closer to her as a team member. As a result, we bonded, and I was far more sensitive to making sure her ideas and concerns were being respected by the entire team. I share this with you as one example of what it means to really connect with someone. She made me see the world differently than I ever had before, and I was the better for it. I had just a taste of what it was like for her living in a white man's world of finance in a leadership position. She made me a better person.

Now I would look at those of a minority status at work and in life as someone I needed to reach out to and make sure I was taking steps to make them feel welcome and included. Before I thought of minorities as people to treat equally; now I looked at minorities as people with whom to engage on a personal as well as professional level. The system was set up for me as a white male. My responsibility was to be sure that I used that system to empower others, especially minorities and women.

Returning to the thoughts on a negotiation and always keeping the end in mind, the key to a successful negotiation is to understand underlying interests. This is often a game-changer in negotiations. Whether in a discussion regarding a major business deal, addressing a conflict at work or home, or managing concerns with a neighbor, the key is to understand their interests. In order to understand interests, solid connecting relationship are helpful, whenever possible.

Earlier you were introduced to the concept of small talk as a way to build connecting relationships. In this chapter this is being taken to another level. Research also has shown that even five minutes of small talk[42] prior to a negotiation results in a better negotiation. Small talk should be just that. It should have nothing to do with the negotiation. The similar commentary may be psychological, political, personal, about the weather or anything else. The key is to find a way to connect with the other individuals. The more you know about the other party the greater the likelihood you can find a way to connect. With such limited time focus on being interested in what they have to say and not so much on being interesting yourself.

Learn More about the Other Party

Gaining information about others can be complicated. You might start by reaching out to your own network. Who has worked or knows something about the other party or people? Learn all you can informally. What are their likes and dislikes? What might be a common area to connect? Your network may offer you some ideas for small talk.

As stated earlier, social media such as Facebook, Twitter, LinkedIn, and others are helpful for business interests. Consider Snapchat, Instagram, Pinterest, YouTube, and others for additional areas of interpersonal connection. There are many more. These are just some ideas for consideration. Consider social networks, discussion forums, blogs, publishing networks and interest-based networks. Think of these as relationship networks.

As a guest lecturer for the last five years at the University of Minnesota's Carlson School of Business, I have been invited to discuss conflict resolution in a Master's level course. I assign students to explore my background on social media and write a one-page paper on how they might try to connect with me. The following week we discuss the results. It is a lot of fun. Now in its fifth year, the assignment sees ever higher quality responses each year, probably a function of the rapid growth of that media. Our shared interests could be brought up in a business setting or a negotiation at breaks, during lunch, or during down times. This process connects my classroom community in surprising ways. We discuss the results and how the results can help them during conflict resolution and negotiations. The bottom line is shared interests help us relate to one another and develop connecting relationships.

Managing Relationships

Managing relationships is about a lot more than simply connecting. It involves communication, consistent interactions, and being transparent. When we are under pressure, we often forgo relationship building and revert to faster, competitive tactics. We take positions rather than focusing on interests. At times this cannot be avoided. But leaders should work to set time aside that can be used to build relationships. This will foster trust going forward. Trust implies honesty, but honesty does not necessarily mean full transparency. Let me explain. In some instances, when working with another party, being honest at all times ensures trust. However, it is not necessarily in your or the other party's best interest to be totally transparent about everything. Total transparency might even cause other concerns.

Here's an example: A firm working on a business deal needed to explain to a second party that certain expenses were related to a potential merger or acquisition with another party. The second party inquired further into those expenses. The firm explained that the expenses were indeed related to the potential merger with or acquisition by another third party. However, they did not explain that the potential third party was management. Management in the firm was also looking into the possibility of buying out the existing owners. That information would have had negative repercussions to the second party wanting to pursue an issue with the firm. As such, the firm explained honestly that the expense was related to the potential acquisition by or merger with a third party, but it was not disclosed that the expense was associated with a possible management takeover of the entity. This allowed the firm and the second party to continue their dialogue and work toward a mutually acceptable resolution regarding the firm and the second party. By first developing a good working relationship (trust but verify[43]) with the other party, the other party can take your word for things that otherwise may have required proof to accept your commentary. In this case the firm was always honest, but not totally transparent. This allowed the process to continue and ultimately led to a conclusion that worked out for everyone. The second party ended up taking over the firm and learned later that management was the third party. This allowed all parties to see each other in a much better light. The key was to always be honest, but not necessarily share everything with the second party.

Often, parties jump right into negotiations or spend only a minimal amount of time building a relationship, listening, and educating. For simple negotiations this can work. If trust already exists, this approach can also work. For more complex negotiations, however, or where parties have no relationship, taking some time to build a connecting relationship from the start can make a real difference. Don't underestimate the need to build and manage good working relationships in a negotiation. They foster trust.

A very successful executive, well-respected by his employees, had responsibilities geographically dispersed over twenty-three states with thousands of employees. I asked him his secret. He told me he always tries to leave time for "management by wandering around." This executive literally walks up to a stranger, introduces himself, and in less than five minutes does the following:

- Introduces himself.
- Asks the other person who they are and what they do at the firm.
- Notes something about the individual based on the personal information in their workstation or work area and comments on it (a photo, a calendar, something on their desk). This allows the other person to share something about themselves.
- Asks if there is anything the person wants to share with him.

He thanks them and leaves. What did he do? In less than five minutes he built at least an initial relationship with someone he did not know at all.

He told me about five percent of the time he hears a golden nugget and about five percent of the time he hears some concern. On the golden nugget he is sure to write a handwritten note to the employee and thank the employee for sharing the insight. Regarding the concern, he knows there always two sides to every issue, so he follows up or has a member of his staff follow up to explore the concern that was brought up. That person explores both sides. He makes sure the employee knows that there was some form of follow up. He indicated to me that ninety percent of the concerns have something to do with communication. As a leader, he wants to make sure the employee is not retaliated against, but instead is recognized for raising the concern. He personally makes sure this takes place. That is a collaborative style of leadership.

How can we apply his example to a negotiation? Take just a few minutes to find a way to connect with someone across the negotiating table. It can go such a long way towards building a better relationship and nurturing trust. Having witnessed this personally and learned from it I have used this same technique in other applications. Asking these kinds of questions allows the questioner to quickly connect with someone. The key is being interested in them and letting them tell you something they want to share.

When managing relationships, don't be afraid of silence. Give yourself and the other party time to think. That's okay. Silence can be our ally. Many negotiators are afraid of silence, but it can be a very powerful form of communication. For example, before you speak you can pause to think and ensure that what you are about to say is stated properly to reflect not only

> In communication, don't be afraid of silence.

the words, but also the tone, body language and facial expressions consistent with your message. The other side will likely pick up on this and realize that you are being very thoughtful. This will likely give additional credibility to your communications. Silence may even cause the other party to make additional concessions.

Negotiate/Mediate/Facilitate with Relationships in Mind

In mediation[44], a mediator facilitates the discussion, and the parties make all the decisions related to their conflict[45]. A mediator is generally brought in after there has been a breakdown in trust and relationships between the parties. The assignment is to assist the parties in finding an amicable solution to their conflict and, often, to avoid litigation. In mediation the parties make the decisions and develop a solution facilitated by the mediator.

As a qualified mediator with the Minnesota Supreme Court, I mediate professionally business to business, business to government, and within businesses. As a volunteer I mediate in Housing Court, Conciliation Court, in public housing, neighborhood disputes, and between gangs.

The process and circumstances can vary significantly. In my professional business I meet with the parties separately ahead of time in order to develop a relationship and trust. The parties can provide confidential information that can be very useful background in the actual mediation. In my volunteer roles that is not the case. I simply have two parties that have agreed to mediate. We have never met before. We simply retreat to a room or do this over Zoom. There is an introduction into the process by me as the mediator, the parties sign a form, and the process is initiated. So how can you build a relationship with both sides in that short time frame?

I was in a situation recently where clearly the parties did not like each other, did not want to be in Housing Court, and were only in mediation to determine when the tenant would move out. It was tense. The tenant wanted to stay until the end of the month. The tenant was already two months behind in rent, wasn't going to pay, and, with no children, could be forcibly evicted in two days. The landlord wanted the tenant out as soon as possible. So why were we in mediation? That was for me to find out. My goal was to build trust with both by being straightforward, accepting of each point of view, being respectful and staying impartial with the process. I asked each "What would you like to have happen?" and then I listened. I asked additional questions clarifying the facts and interests. The emotions were high. By listening actively and slowing down the discussion, the tenant indicated additional things he was willing to do if he could remain until the end of the month; his offer included fixing some items, cleaning the place, and leaving in civil manner. This was important to the landlord too. The landlord knew that the tenant had alternatives for shelter by the end of the month, but would otherwise be homeless. It was February in Minnesota. This could be life-threatening. The parties agreed on specific terms. I wrote it up. They each signed the agreement. It was brought before the court and was entered as the official agreement. Even with limited time together, a smile, a professional demeanor, a caring attitude, being respectful of each party, being interested in being fair with the parties goes a long way for the mediator to build trust in a very short period of time. You can do this too. Even in trying circumstances.

While relationships and trust are important, there are also strategies in mediation. There are three types of mediation. One type is evaluative. This technique is often conducted by a retired judge or an attorney who has listened to all the facts and then advises the parties as to what he or she thinks may happen should the case go to court. A second type is facilitative mediation, in which the mediator focuses on a particular problem and works with the parties to find a solution acceptable to both parties. The third type is transformative mediation. In transformative mediation, the mediator's primary focus is to actually change the relationship of the parties. With facilitative or transformative mediation, the mediator meets with the parties separately before the mediation to develop trust, listen to their concerns, and look for ways to bring the parties together during the mediation process. Connecting with the parties is key.

The same techniques are used in formal negotiations and in a business setting. Taking the time to share some personal and/or professional information before diving into the dispute by asking the other party if they would be willing to share some things about themselves to develop trust at the outset can be very helpful.

In situations where the parties know each other, having an ice breaker or something fun can lighten the stage and increase the possibilities of success from the outset. When you work with others day to day and know a lot about each other the ice breaker can help break any tension.

Summary

In this chapter, the focus was on connecting relationships. It takes genuine work to build relationships and manage them positively. Central to that effort is communicating with the other person to uncover hidden interests and sharing some of your own. Small talk can be very useful even if all you have is very limited time. Listening actively demonstrates interest in the other party. The story of the successful executive demonstrates that even a small investment of time can build new relationships and even help the entire enterprise. My story of connecting with a colleague in Washington, D.C. points to the way interpersonal relationships can be built by teams. Even in difficult circumstances with formal negotiations, taking the time to get to know the other party participants can result in better communication, which, in turn, can bring satisfactory or even better outcomes. The basic techniques associated with negotiation, mediation, and facilitation are useful in multiple settings.

Chapter 6

LISTENING ACTIVELY

*"One of the most sincere forms of respect is actually
listening to what another has to say."*
—Byrant H. McGill

This is probably the most important chapter in this book. The title implies such a simple act—listening actively. Close your mouth to be an outstanding listener. But it doesn't just happen. You have to be conscious of listening to keep yourself from sharing what you want to say before listening. You need to really listen to the other party. That sounds easy, too. It's not. But this chapter seeks to show you that the difficult is possible. The best communicators know when to keep their mouths closed and really listen. Rather than trying to promote themselves, an idea, or a position, they focus on trying to understand others first.

Sometimes, each of us simply wants to be heard. That is a different situation. Here the emphasis is simply to listen and help the party sort out a solution. A lot has been written on how to actively listen in a negotiation[46] and how to listen better with difficult people[47]. Sometimes it's easy with people we really care about and we want to hear what they have to say. Other times it is very difficult, especially when we want to bring across something we feel strongly about. In these situations, listening takes work and conscious effort. When all you want to do is let the other party know what you are thinking, and what you want them to do, it is especially difficult to listen. However, if you really want to communicate your message, listen.

When you present the critical facts in a discussion, a presentation, or a negotiation leave a sufficient amount of time for questions and answers. This allows you additional time for listening to the other party's concerns. Consider bringing on board a facilitator whose purpose is to encourage listening and make sure everyone is heard. Have someone take notes and read them back after the meeting to make sure others know their ideas had been taken seriously. Imagine that as a style of leadership. A leader who listens is perceived much better than one who tries to demonstrate that he or she has all the answers and speaks over others.

Paraphrase, Summarize, Use Open-Ended Questions, and Empathize

There is a strategy to effective listening. This doesn't just happen. You have to be conscious and take deliberate actions to listen actively. Listening actively requires you to paraphrase, summarize, ask open-ended questions, and empathize. Paraphrase means to use different words than the speaker used, but to clearly articulate your interpretation of what was said. Summarizing is presenting the major points on what you just heard. Your goal is to apply both paraphrasing and summarizing to clearly demonstrate that you heard what was said and can present it, perhaps more concisely than the presenter. That is an excellent way to demonstrate active listening. Along the way ask open ended questions to obtain clarification. This shows a genuine interest. Open ended questions help you understand and allows the other party to see that you really have understood.

Here are open ended questions and follow up ideas for you to consider:

- What would you like to have happen? (this is my favorite question in a mediation/negotiation).
- What is your story?
- What are you working on lately?
- What is your passion?
- What is really bothering you?
- What are your worst fears?
- Tell me more about yourself/ your business.
- Tell me more.

Finally, listen with empathy. That is, share that you understand their feelings. Sympathy means to share the pain. Empathy means to feel the pain that leads to taking action. Instead, focus on understanding. Demonstrate your concern for the feelings of the other party.

Even if the other party is not listening as effectively to you, by you listening to them, you will likely enhance their ability to be more open minded to your perspective. Keep this in mind even if they are not acknowledging what you are saying. Listening effectively with empathy really works in a negotiation.

Research shows that attitude and feelings in communication is attributed 7% to the words, 38% to the tone, and 55% to the facial expression and body language of the person speaking[48]. Note that this observation is not relevant to all conversations; rather these are generalizations. Specific conversations may have varying percentages. Experts suggest that people experience the best understanding of the attitude behind a communication when it is face to face, and the least understanding from a text or an email.

Understanding generational differences is also important. As a Baby Boomer, I am oriented towards face to face communication as my preferred approach. However, my millennial children prefer texts. Some millennials I know feel so strongly about this mode of communication that they keep their phone completely filled with messages so there is no room to leave a message. This preference is obvious but disconcerting, given that they are sufficiently behind in responding to other messages that they are willing to miss newer ones. This example points out the need to modify your behavior and to adjust to the need of the other party to be a better listener. If we really need to talk, I may need to text an individual and request a call. That works. Adjust your thinking to that of the party to enhance communications.

Early in my career, I managed a group of one woman and eight men. Later, I took a new position where I managed a team of six women with only one man. About two weeks into this new job, I knew something wasn't quite right. I just didn't know what the problem was. One day I decided to ask one of my employees, Gail, when she entered my office to seek her advice. I said to her "Gail, I feel that something isn't quite right, but I can't put my finger on it. Do you have any ideas?" Gail's face turned a little red and then she looked down at the floor for a moment. Slowly, she raised her head and quietly said, "Well, sometimes when we come in your office, we just want you to listen." I thought about what she said for a few moments, we talked about it for a little while, and I thanked her for her honesty and comment. I offered that maybe I could bring this up at a group meeting. She concurred. At the next group meeting I brought it up. It was a bit awkward. I think maybe they felt sorry for me as a newer manager, but they were willing to work with me. We worked the issue and the group came up with a plan. If someone came to my office door, knocked on the side of the door frame, and used the code word "blue," that meant they wanted me to listen. We decided to test out our new approach.

When the first person came and knocked on my door and said "blue," I took immediate action. I pushed away from my desk and computer and rolled my chair to a small round table in the corner of my office. I grabbed a pad of paper and a pen, ready to take notes. My employee sat down at the table, and I simply listened by summarizing, paraphrasing, asking open-ended questions, and empathizing. I did not provide any solutions. I may have asked questions that led in a given direction, but did not provide a solution; listening was key.

What I discovered is 9 out of 10 times they figured out how to resolve their issue on their own. They felt good about this, and remembered the lesson they had learned themselves. I was amazed how well this technique worked. As a newer manager it actually cut down on how many questions my employees brought to me. I had thought that I had to have all the answers as a newer manager. As their confidence grew and they figured out answers themselves this helped reduce the burden on me too. For me, this was money in the bank. It was an "ah ha" moment that changed my career. I was so excited by what I had learned about listening actively that when I came home, I told my wife all about it. She looked at me and said, "You can do that home too." I laughed. This powerful lesson has stayed with me my whole career and deepened my relationship with my wife. Active listening is critical.

Since then, I have learned a generalization from neuroscience. Men tend to listen to solve a problem and come up with a solution. Women tend to listen to understand. I had to really focus on listening to understand in order to become a better manager and listener. This has helped me my entire career, all the way to the executive suite. You can apply this lesson on listening at work, at home and in your life. You may be surprised at what you learn from the experience.

Be a team player. Do be a team member and team player. Don't be aloof or condescending, a sure-fire way to shut down interaction. Don't interrupt, even when you think you know where the conversation is going and have a response. Listening is very difficult. I know this all too well, personally; I do tend to interrupt. It is hard for me. Be there to learn. Be there to understand. Be present in the moment with the other party. Stay calm and control the fire within, if you are angry or emotional. When things are going well, shine a spotlight on the situation. Let people have their time in the sun. Direct positive energy to the person being honored. Give them positive affirmation.

Find Common Ground through Values

When given a laundry list of concerns, determine which are most critical and address those first. Identify clearly what is of the greatest importance and don't get bogged down in the minutia. If something is determined to be less critical, accept the assessment and move on to items that truly matter to the task at hand. Focus on values and not on beliefs. This is very important. Even in the most serious of discussions, look for common values. Don't focus on individual beliefs. By focusing on common values, disputants may find it possible to listen to each other even in very trying circumstances. One of the most fraught contemporary topics is abortion, but I have seen a circumstance in which two sides came to a kind of shared value. You know where each side was coming from when I mention the word. However, when both sides focused on unwanted pregnancies and raising children in a loving home, that shifted the parties to focus on what they had in common focusing on values.

> Focus on values and not on beliefs

You will not convince someone to change their minds on something they believe in very strongly. However, you may be able to relate to their point of view by finding common values. Learning to look for common values facilitates conflict resolution and understanding.

It is our tendency to arrive ready to do battle. Work to de-escalate yourself[49]. Instead of being there to tell the other party what you want to say, listen to them and their concerns. Ask them "What is it they want to have happen?" Avoid being provoked into a negative response. Don't abandon value-creating strategies. Use time to your advantage. Be there to listen. Realize this takes a real effort. This doesn't just happen. Be quiet and listen.

In general, it is useful to calm yourself. Consider mediation, prayer, or reflection for at least 10 minutes daily[50]. Studies[51] have shown carrying out this simple technique for as little as 30 days[52] can lower your blood pressure[53] and help you calm the fire by being able to control your triggers[54] when you begin to feel yourself beginning to become angry. Long term studies[55] point to even healthier long-term impacts. Mindfulness[56] really works to help calm us. You can start with as little as five minutes a day[57]. Both the Greater Good Science Center at the University of California at Berkeley[58] and the course on Happiness at Yale[59] present evidence that taking the time for mindfulness at least 10 minutes a day produces more happiness in participants.

Keep in mind no one is perfect at interpreting facial or body language[60], but there are steps you can take to gain more control over your own body language. There are also steps you can take to improve your interpretation and understanding of others' body language. This can be critical in a negotiation. Your body language takes on a similar form to the other party when you are both on the same page. That is, if the other party leans in and smiles you tend to lean in and smile too. Think of your interactions with friends.

Have you ever noticed if a person in a negotiation crosses their legs? Did you tend to cross your legs too? If someone is relaxed and leans back in their chair, do you tend to do the same? There is a reason for this: When we are comfortable with others, we tend to take on the same body language.

It turns out if the other party is positive and warm there is a 95% chance our response will be the same. Unfortunately, the same is true for a negative response. If the other party is negative, stay focused on the problem, stay above the line, and remain positive and professional. Mirror body language when it is positive or neutral. Negative thoughts will result in facial expressions and body language that will present a negative response and deteriorate into escalation rather than de-escalation.

Think about the importance of this nugget of wisdom in a negotiation. If you adopt similar body language to the other party, that could promote comfort and relaxation in the meeting. The negotiations may become more fluid and dynamic as a result. This may lead to improved listening. Upon discovering interests, it may be possible to work together to address each other's interests. Think how being conscious of your full demeanor can help with a negotiation.

Practice Patience and Professionalism

We all know the advantage to remaining calm under pressure. We may look calm on the outside, but inside we might be churning. You may put your happy face on while inside you are angry, frustrated, or irritated. Even if you think you're a good actor, your facial expressions and body language might be giving you away. Be careful. Researchers have found when we give answers that are not genuine, we display inconsistent facial expressions. We blink more. That's one reason why it's difficult to maintain a lie. You may have a hard time hiding your true feelings. The same is true for others.

Understand cultural differences. Don't apply your culture or assume norms. When working with a different culture, reach out to others[61]. Expand your horizons. Bring in help.

Mediating in New York on Western Long Island, I witnessed two parties as they used the F- bomb word very loosely with each other. This was simply their way of speaking. As the mediator, I simply asked if the parties—having agreed to be professional with each other and to treat each other with respect —were ok with this language. They agreed they were. It was necessary for me to adjust to their way of thinking, words, and tone. They were comfortable with being able to relax into the discussion. Understand who you are working with and their perspective. All of these comments associated with negotiation are directly on point to listening actively. In chapter 8, additional insights will be provided regarding negotiation techniques.

As with any negotiation, practice is the key. Think about what you need to do to prepare[62] for the negotiation. Meet with your team and go over how you believe the negotiation may proceed. Discuss all the various questions you may want to consider. Focus on how you will make sure you are listening. Circle back and ensure understanding by summarizing key points before moving on to the next topic.

Look at this check list[63] from the Harvard Law School Program on Negotiations. It offers great questions to ask before going into any negotiation. Personally, I would encourage you to use this as a starting point and over time develop your own checklists and handouts.

In any anticipated negotiation, think about relevant questions ahead of time regarding your team considering listening. Who may respond? How will that person or you interact? Think about the ramifications ahead of time. If you are working with a team, have a plan to address who will be involved with particular topics. You may have a simple plan, but give it real thought. Practice ahead of time and develop alternatives with an idea about who will address what during the negotiation process. In the end, take yourself seriously, but not too seriously, and that will allow you to be creative. Once the negotiation commences, use the outline with perhaps some alternative ideas that can be adopted as circumstances change is useful. These sessions rarely go as planned, but having planned ahead of time will give you the flexibility to adapt to the situation.

From your own experiences, you know that in an argument you like being heard. The same is true for the other party. There are benefits derived from truly validating the other party in an argument. Listen to your opponent before speaking yourself. Take the lead and listen. Let them know that they made a good point. Compliment them on their patience. Thank them for some insight.

In Western culture and debate, students are taught to start preparing their response while the other side is still speaking. This is done to be ready to respond as soon as the other side finishes their commentary. Formal debaters are evaluated by how well they address and refute each of the points made by the other side—all with strict time constraints. That is not how to listen actively to connect with others when you are seeking a common solution. Given this background, what is being presented here runs totally contrary to what you may have been taught in debate or what you may have gleaned from watching TV legal dramas. To win in a negotiation, reframe, reaffirm, and restate what you understand from the other side. Validate what they have said before proceeding further.

> Listen to your opponent before speaking yourself. Take the lead and listen. Let them know that they made a good point. Compliment them on their patience. Thank them for some insight.

Instead of trying to refute the other side, validate their concerns.[64] Let them know you are listening. Summarize what they say. This demonstrates active listening. Understand this and work with this in a negotiation. Remember it is up to you to model good communication behavior before you take action

Neuroscience[65] tells us that if we focus on remaining calm and listening to the other party, we can work towards a successful resolution with that party, but we need to focus on the decision-maker.

Keep in mind who the ultimate decision-maker is. This is especially needed in a negotiation. Good negotiators know this and make a point to validate the other party and their perspective. Hopefully, you have a decision-maker in the session. This may not always be the case. Understand and clarify the limitations of the person you are interacting with. For example, if this is not the ultimate decision-maker, you need to clarify this from the very beginning. Understand this person's authority. If none, this likely needs to be a brief informative session only. If the person has some authority, clarify what that means and proceed accordingly. If this person has full authority, proceed knowing you have the right person involved. You need to know that the other party has the authority to make decisions from the very beginning to not waste time for either party.

You have probably noticed that you enjoy conversations with others that listen to you more than they speak. They seem to have a genuine interest in you, and they seem to care. Applying this technique with others you may even begin to develop a relationship and enhance trust with the other party. This can be transformative. Small talk can further enhance understanding while expanding your relationship with the other party.

Summary

Since most people do not listen well and really do not intend to understand, this chapter can be extremely helpful. Most people listen with the intention to reply or to be interesting. In this chapter you learned to focus on being interested in the other party. It is more important to be interested than to be interesting. You were given tools to be a proactive listener. To do this you need to summarize, paraphrase, ask open ended questions and empathize. By listening for what is important and calming your internal fire you will enhance your listening capabilities. Understanding how words, tone and the combination of facial expression and body language impact listening is critical. With practice and patience in application, you will enhance your own professionalism. By following the other party's lead and applying insights in this chapter from neuroscience, you can become a much better listener and conversationalist. You do this by validating the other side.

Chapter 7

EDUCATING JUDICIOUSLY

"A good expert doesn't just explain their findings, they make a connection ... that conveys trust and credibility."
—Ava Lawson

E ducating judiciously is the third step of The Collaboration Effect. Most parties to a conflict believe they know their own position and interests. At a minimum, they know their own starting point. For example, in sales, they know their product and pricing. In litigation they know their facts and legal arguments before going to court. In a tough negotiation, in general they know both their and the other party's positions pretty well. Good negotiators have prepared thoroughly and they have studied the backgrounds of the other parties involved. In other words, they have a lot of information at their disposal. However, educating judiciously is actually about

> Educating judiciously is actually about saying or providing just the necessary information at any given point in time the way the other party would like to be educated.

saying or providing just the necessary information at any given point in time the way the other party would like to be educated. It is crucial not to overwhelm the other party with extraneous information that could cloud the conversation or distract from the task at hand. Many people overshare—they simply can't help themselves—and they overwhelm decision-makers with too much information. This can distract all the stakeholders and negatively impact outcomes.

As stated previously, doing research on the other party to build a connection, listening actively, and being prepared[66] are keys for effective collaboration in a negotiation. In the last chapter, you learned how to listen actively using the techniques of summarizing, paraphrasing, asking open ended questions, and being empathetic. You saw how these skills played a critical role in successful conflict resolution and negotiation. These techniques set the stage for the other party to be able to listen to you, so incorporate all of these techniques before beginning to educate the other party. As neuroscience tells us, listen first to be understood.[67] Once someone has been listened to, they are far more likely to listen back. To negotiate successfully, you need to educate judiciously, taking into account your and their interests.

Explore Your Own Interests

Start by exploring your own interests in a negotiation. While it is tempting to get right to the point, you may not stop and take the time to consider anything beyond the most obvious issues. For example, it may be about money as an obvious point of contention. However, upon further consideration, the participants may also be concerned about other interests. For example, closure, and an ongoing relationship, as well as others' perceptions (clients, vendors, shareholders, employees, customers, regulators, and other interested parties) of fairness. The final solution may involve a delivery date, designation of who will deliver what in the process, the quality of the product or service, the potential for future products or services, attention to additional relationships, and other considerations. Explore your goals, values[68] and interests, and consider how these will play out in a collaboration or a negotiation.

Know Your Strengths and Weaknesses

Before working on educating others, it pays to know your own strengths and weaknesses[69], and you may want to bring others with you to ensure you have the strongest team possible. We tend to know our own strengths, but maybe not our weaknesses. That may require asking others to help us identify our weaknesses. Consider identifying your strengths and weaknesses[70]. You can leverage your strengths and potentially improve on your weaknesses. In the near term, you may be ahead to bring someone or others with you that can address your weaknesses.

It can be helpful to understand both the strengths and weaknesses associated with your personality type. Myers Briggs testing[71] provides one of 16 combinations associated with introversion – extroversion, intuitive – sensing, thinking – feeling, and judging – perceiving. Just exploring the category of judging the plus side is being able to decide quickly and fairly by being decisive. The negative side of judging can be reaching a decision too quickly, possibly not considering others' feelings, and not involving others. Knowing this, a person with the ability to judge quickly may want to bring someone with them that is more perceptive and can suggest taking a break and considering the feelings and perceptions of others before making a decision. A good leader appreciates that spectrum and avoids going to

> By surrounding yourself with others that compliment your weaknesses this enhances the probability of success.

extremes. Understanding your own perspective and identifying those of others can lead to better decisions. By surrounding yourself with others that compliment your weaknesses this enhances the probability of success.

Their insights can help you make a better decision. They can bring up questions and concerns that you had not thought of or anticipated. Knowing your strengths and weaknesses you can work on addressing your weaknesses.

Let's start with what educate judiciously does <u>not</u> mean. It does not mean that you should be arrogant or pompous, as that can backfire. For example, in court proceedings many expert witnesses are told that they should not advocate for their client. Instead, they should advocate for their position. This sounds great in theory. In reality, though, this approach can discount an expert witness's testimony. An egotistical or pompous expert can work against the client by not providing the court with credible testimony. Many experts need to be educated to think about how to relate to the judge and jury and thus gain their confidence. Being able to relate to those making decisions is essential.

An expert witness who can provide information in a straightforward manner—with professionalism, honesty, and integrity—is a great asset. If he or she is friendly, reliable, knowledgeable, open, transparent, and accepting of others, this will go a long way towards promoting trust—and we all know the power of trust.

The expert witness should not oversell his or her ideas or promote self-interest. They are present to explain things in a way that the other party can understand. They are there to clarify, so that the other party can accept the information and facts being presented. You want to encourage the other side to want to know more.

A judicious approach typically means taking a broad view rather than a narrow focus. This means weighing the facts in an even-handed manner and exploring the various issues and underlying interests. Knowing the audience is key. The way one speaks to a child is very different than the way one speaks to a graduate class in a specific area of study. A clear understanding of the audience can allow an expert witness to provide relevant commentary and help the other party grasp the context and meaning of information.

Your attitude is critical. You are there to help. You are there to listen. Your goal is to facilitate both the other party or the decider of fact to make a good decision based on all of the facts laid out in a manner that is clearly understood.

Educate in this instance means to inform. To take advantage of The Collaboration Effect, education means more than simply sharing information. It means understanding the interests of the other party and based on those interests, providing information that will either ease their pain or provide them with better outcomes.

If the other party doesn't care, they won't listen. The goal is to help them realize that they should care, by educating them in a way they prefer to be educated. This might be visual, auditory, or kinesthetic. We all have different learning styles[72]. Knowing the other party's preferred learning style and adapting to their needs can pay big dividends.

Educating is emotional. Since our brains are 98% emotional and 2% rational[73], it's crucial to address the emotional side of the brain while educating people. This may be done with stories, facts coupled with emotional insights, and by reaching out to the interests of the other party that were uncovered during listening actively. Rather than simply

> Since our brains are 98% emotional and 2% rationale[73], it's crucial to address the emotional side of the brain while educating people.

presenting facts, consider an emotional perspective while educating the other party.

Think about it. If you were working with a financial planner and your biggest concerns were to have enough money for your children's' education and your retirement, you would likely be more receptive if you knew what it would take to meet those needs rather than if you were told you would have "X" dollars in 20 or 30 years. Yes, it is nice to know the dollar amount, but it is even more compelling to see that your financial planner has a sense of how this money will impact your wellbeing and future. In this case, the financial planner identified two central needs: the client's children's education and retirement savings. When those two emotional needs were satisfied, the party was educated judiciously.

My own experience with two financial planners can demonstrate why listening judiciously and communicating effectively is so central. Before I interviewed these planners, my wife asked me to do the interviewing and then come back to her with the highlights before we made any decision. Knowing that with my MBA in finance I would likely have much to say, she indicated she would prefer the abbreviated version of those interactions. It was instructive to see how each of these financial planners addressed educating judiciously differently. Each were great at building connecting relationships. They also excelled when it came to listening actively. However, when it came to the educating judiciously, these financial planners made some fundamental errors that are useful as counter examples to effective educating.

The initial contact with the first Certified Financial Planner, CFP, was exceptional. He was great at building connecting relationships and listening actively. This CFP introduced me to his boss, the Director of Financial Planning. After that handover I never heard another word from the CFP. He was present at all of the future meetings, but besides welcoming me we had no other interaction. The Director spent no time connecting with me. He was all business. He wanted me to know all about him, his firm and how great they were for their clients. It was clear the Director's role was to educate the client and close the deal. From the start of these interactions it was clear to me that this is what the Director presented for every client. I indicated that I had a background in finance, and I would not need the full commentary in all areas. This was ignored by the Director who insisted that I needed to sit through a painfully descriptive presentation of everything on his list. He did not legally have to provide everything he provided. This was simply his style and took no extra effort on his part. All I wanted was an overview, but my request was not respected by the Director. He was not able to alter his presentation. He did not appear to know or care to alter his presentation. He could not customize what was needed for the individual client. This clearly turned me off. He knew his stuff, but he provided me with more than I cared to have him orally present. I was happy to read the information and resented the time he took to cover material that was not necessary.

In a second instance, a Director I met with kept repeating information during three follow-up sessions related to educating the client. Each time the Director opened a session, it was clear he did not know where he had left off during the last presentation. And each time, I would remind the manager that he had already covered these sections. Unruffled, the Director would simply indicate that he thought the information was worthy of another review. This wasted my time and I found it irritating. Although I remained respectful, I was clearly not impressed by the Director's approach. He presented too much information and repeated himself. It seemed like the education sessions were going to go on forever. There was no end in sight. To me it appeared that that the Director thought that by keeping me coming back for more sessions he would eventually wear me down, so that I would capitulate and sign on the bottom line for the financial firm's services. Not only was this approach ineffective, it completely backfired. I was exhausted by the inefficiency of the process. In the end I thanked the CFP and the Director for their due diligence and I indicated that their services would not be needed. I took my voting dollars elsewhere.

All three elements of The Collaboration Effect are critical. Though they are each distinct, they are all intertwined and require careful planning to build effective bridges to negotiate closure. In the financial planner examples, the firm lost the client because they failed to actively listen and educate judiciously during the closure phase. You can learn from their mistakes. Connect with your prospects and clients. Listen to them in order to understand what they want to learn from you. Provide limited information and ask them plenty of open-ended questions. Educate them on their own terms. Focus on not speaking and instead listen to them. Then modify your approach to address their concerns and interests.

When I am recounting a family story, my daughter often nudges me and says, "Dad, land the plane." It's her gentle way of reminding me to wrap up the story, as I tend to go on for too long. I get it. I embellish. I provide too much detail. I get sidetracked and go off on too many tangents.

I need to take my own advice and clue into to what my audience wants to hear. I may have a lot I want to say, but if you are listening and want closure, well, then it's time for me to wrap it up.

Sometimes you just have to not say anything and simply listen. By talking less and listening more during this educational phase you may obtain additional unexpected insights. Even when you are answering questions, be brief unless the listener indicates that they want more detail—normally they don't.

Have the mindset to serve and then just listen. This simple technique has worked well for me when I meet a potential new client. I share a little bit about my background, let them know who my clients are, and how they have benefited...then I start asking questions and listening. You can try this too. The results can be surprising. Continue to apply the techniques of The Collaboration Effect and you are quite likely to develop a number of true friendships and long-term clients.

Educate Judiciously Based on What You Want

Before going further, pause and consider what it is that you really want. Most people want to know that they can trust you, you are knowledgeable, and that they can see how you add value in order to want to collaborate with you. Start out educating judiciously by exploring their level of interest. You are ready to educate, and you have a lot to say, but think about these three elements before proceeding further.

To help you I want to share with you three steps from John Baker's book, The Asking Formula[74]. In a nutshell he indicates that to be successful you have to address these three elements:

1. Know what I want.
2. Ask for it.
3. Have three reasons as to why this is beneficial for the other party.

Looking at the third element, consider your three best reasons and develop them well before presenting them.

For example, being on a nominating committee for the church council, I thought about how to persuade a busy member of the congregation to take on council membership for a three-year term.

1. You are a caring, competent, concerned faithful member of this congregation who would be an ideal candidate for the church council given your background.
2. As a member of the church council you have an opportunity to bring your leadership skills and enhance your skills while making a genuine difference in the life of this congregation.
3. You would gain real insight into how and why this congregation runs so smoothly and what we bring to each other, the community, and the world with our faithful stewardship.

You can apply this sample in a wide range of other settings. Prepare ahead with very specific arguments about why someone should hire you or your firm, buy what you are selling, collaborate with you, or work with you to resolve a conflict. Focus on three things that differentiate you and how you add value distinct from your competition. Focus on the end game. Be sure to get to the point quickly and then listen to their questions to educate judiciously. Since you already developed a connecting relationship, listened actively, using this technique to educate judiciously allows you to address their concerns. This same technique can be applied in sales, in a discussion with your boss, reaching out to a peer, working with a subordinate, or interacting with someone else. Think about what you are going to say ahead of time regarding what you want.

1. Know what I want.
2. Ask for it.
3. Have three best reasons as to why this is beneficial for the other party.

Having conducted over 2,500 mediations, negotiations, and facilitations throughout my career, I know how to put this technique into action. I encourage you to take the ideas in this book and discuss them with your team. Understand the top three incentives that will motivate someone else before entering into any negotiation. That was the purpose of listening.

In many business conflicts, the attorneys have written several-hundred-page brief with dozens of points. That's great, but the decision-makers on both sides are not going to read and understand all of the nuances of that document. Instead, they'll follow the 80-20 Pareto principle[75], which states "for many events, roughly 80% of the effects come from 20% of the causes."

Keep this in mind for your own commentary. Educate judiciously even in very complex legal battles. Often even very complex legal battles turn on a few major points. Dozens of minor issues can typically be boiled down to two or three major issues.

People like the rule of three[76], so focus on your three best reasons and state those up front.

The rest can be stored in an appendix or brief and called up when needed. By focusing on your three best points, you will avoid overwhelming the other side or the decision-maker. As a result, the other party may have the mental capacity to ask you questions about the other items that you have not introduced as part of your three major points. What you want is for the other side to be curious and to ask you questions. In that way you are engaging them. You are helping them to be interested. You are answering their concerns and may well then be able to build in those other points you had identified and that appear in the appendix. Further inquiry about your perspective is exactly what you want to have happen. This is what you were hoping for in order to move towards closure.

Summary

In this chapter the focus is on how to educate judiciously by adapting what you want to say to the way in which the recipient wants to hear the information. An emphasis is on exploring your own interests and reshaping them in response to others. Explore your strengths and weaknesses and where possible include others that can help you overcome your weaknesses. Understand what educating and judiciously mean and don't mean. Learn from the examples from the two directors from the financial firms on what not to do. Don't take over. Be conscious of the other party's time. Focus on closure from the beginning. Know what you want. Ask for it. Have three good reasons why it is in the other party's best interest. Then listen and work with the other party.

Chapter 8

BUILDING BRIDGES TO CLOSURE

"Many ideas grow better when transplanted into another mind than the one where they sprang up."
—Oliver Wendell Holmes

Think about the tactics you will use from the beginning to the end in a negotiation. This book is designed to set you up for success. By applying techniques in these chapters, you will be able to influence the outcome and protect yourself as you focus on finding solutions and bringing closure to all the participants. You can explore other books for additional insights on negotiation[77]. This chapter applies The Collaboration Effect to negotiate closure.

A most important issue to address is who will represent each side in the negotiation. You want to have decision-makers at the table. These are individuals who have the authority to make a decision on behalf of their side. They will be critical as you move

> You want to have decision-makers at the table.

the process forward. You also want individuals that point out potential concerns. This is very important. However, you want to avoid participants that can become entrenched focusing only on positions.

Where you meet is often significant. It can be at your location. It can be at the other party's location. You could meet at a neutral location. Depending on the negotiation, location may not matter. Sometimes, though, to ensure even-handedness, a neutral location may be necessary. Face-to-face interactions are still best for difficult negotiations. In today's world these may need to be completed virtually. If that is the case consider "The Art of Virtual Mediation," chapter 10 in my book Peaceful Resolutions.[78] You can explore video conferencing with platforms like Zoom, Skype, Teams, or other services. Given travel costs, this may be a viable alternative. However, even with video conferencing, some of the benefits of in-person meetings, discussed in chapter 10, are lost when body language is not fully visible. When making that decision about virtual meetings, you must weigh the pros and cons, personal safety, and the importance of the negotiation.

For example, with virtual meetings you need to consider:

- Making eye contact with the webcam
- Using open-handed gestures
- Orienting your body towards the camera
- Nodding your head occasionally while listening
- Sitting upright while occasionally leaning forward
- Ensuring each party participates from a quiet location to limit interruptions, interference, and distractions
- Avoiding fidgeting, playing with jewelry, or your hair
- Avoiding frequent touching of your face and your clothing
- Being prepared and confident—this helps ensure tone and paralanguage is positive
- Dressing suitably, the same you would for a face-to-face process

- Ensuring quality video and audio
- Better protection of the party's privacy
- Better support for mobile devices—iPad, iPhone, android, smart phone, tablets

Dates and time of day for a negotiation are also significant. Select a time that works well for everyone concerned. Explore the various participants' perspectives relative to timing because some may have personal issues that are not visible but important to them. Consider time-zone differences, too. You may recall the story at the beginning of this book, and the how important it was to know when the meeting took place and the duration of the meeting. The parties preferred a morning meeting and they doubled the time they thought they needed for the meeting to make sure they addressed everyone's needs. It was also important to build a mutual agenda and leave time for food and restroom breaks. As indicated earlier, have appropriate food and beverages conducive to a negotiation.

Negotiators should start the meeting asking the parties if they want to have any ground rules. If so ask them for specific requirements and expectations. This is a first step towards working collaboratively on something together. Work with your own team to enforce these ground rules. Work with the other party to mutually develop an agenda. Don't just show up and hope it works. This is setting yourself up for potential failure. By being proactive with your own team as well as the other party you can increase your probability of success. Knowing pre-identified participants, their titles, and their roles is important, but also leave time for introductions and sharing backgrounds to break the ice. Make use of what you have learned about connecting relationships, listening actively, and educating judiciously as you work into the negotiations. Encourage all parties to be truthful, honest, forthright, and professional while speaking one at a time and not interrupting each other.

Enhancing Value through Additional Techniques

It is always easier to assume we are right and the other side is wrong. In many negotiations the parties begin by assuming they are right (or mostly right) and the other side is the party that must concede. Our minds prefer binary decisions—right versus wrong. We also like to think we are right and the other party is wrong.

When I make presentations, I often ask my audiences, "How many sides are there to a coin?" Some will respond with an answer of "two sides" and others will respond with an answer of "three sides". The next Power Point slide shows a few coins close up. Clearly there is a head side, a tail side and a third circular side to the coin. Then I state,

"Similarly, in a negotiation there are three sides. My side, your side and the truth."

The question is what is the truth? That is the question before us. What is the truth? This is complex. The truth may never be found. Reaching an acceptable solution to both parties is the goal. The solution is something both sides can live with. The closer we can approach the truth the greater the likelihood we may be able to reach an agreement. "

This tells me that we should be focused on trying to determine the truth. Both parties should enter the negotiating process with an open mind in which not only the bottom line but also the opposing party's interests are taken into consideration. This approach can be very positive on having both parties move towards an acceptable resolution. Now the emphasis is on influencing the outcome.

Consider how you approach each issue in a negotiation. Make sure your own attitude and position on the issue are appropriate. Be positive. Have an open mind. Be there to help. Focus not so much on being understood, but on understanding. Think about how you want to present the issue. Consider how you might be perceived by the other party. Focus on presenting how you can help them best to understand. Be confident, but don't be pompous. Be open to listening.

Make use of various persuasive techniques such as silence, appreciation, and disappointment. Each of these can have a tremendous impact in a negotiation. If someone were to ask you a question, you might consider what must be going through their heads as you sit silently and contemplate your understanding. Think response. They may even blurt out something or offer something simply to overcome the silence. Silence can give the other party pause and may lead them to offer additional information.

You like positive reinforcement and so do they. Look for opportunities to give positive reinforcement. Statements such as "That is a really good question", "That is very insightful on your part", "I am glad you brought that up", "Thank you for that suggestion", "I am glad you're here", "Bringing up that point is very helpful" can be very reaffirming. Look for ways to catch the other party doing something right and let them know you appreciate what they did and that you appreciate them.

If they present something that indeed is very disappointing, consider whether to bring it up or not. If it was disappointing and bringing it up may be negative, maybe you can let it pass. On the other hand, if things are moving along positively and, suddenly, they bring up something negative that may dampen negotiations, expressing your disappointment may put things back on track. For example, if the other party brought up something negative from earlier in the negotiations that you feel you have moved beyond at this point you might say something like, "We have already worked through that issue. I thought that the issue was closed and that we have moved on. I am disappointed that you have brought this up again. Might I suggest that we stay focused on the current issue in front of us so that we can determine together how to address this issue going forward?"

Consider reaching out to others that have additional experience or insights related to this negotiation or to negotiations in general. Reach out to your mentors. In the course of this book, many ideas have been presented for your consideration. We are all shaped by our experiences. Reaching out to others that have had more or broader experiences may be very helpful if you don't have as much experience about particular issues. If things are not going well, consider your Best Alternative to a Negotiated Agreement (BATNA); that is, if we don't at least make it to our BATNA we are prepared to walk away. Having developed your position and your BATNA, develop three other alternatives between your position and your BATNA. Have these computed ahead of time for potential offers during the negotiation, and that will allow you either to use these or to pivot and offer something else based on having done your homework.

Throw out the first anchor[79]. An anchor is the first offer by a party in a negotiation. Often throwing out the first anchor, say, your lowest of the three alternatives, can set the stage for the negotiations. The anchor needs to be well-reasoned, fair and take into consideration the interests of the other party. Studies [80]have shown that the party that makes the first offer can have a significant impact on the outcome.

Ask the other party what they think about the offer. Listen actively. Ask open-ended questions. Make sure they feel heard. Use the techniques presented earlier on listening actively. Keep in mind that not everybody plays fair. You need to take steps to protect yourself from those that don't play fair.

Protecting Yourself

Not everyone plays fair. Some negotiations are with difficult people[81]. They threaten, lie, deceive, or bully. Keep in mind those that bully and that take unethical approaches may reflect underlying personal problems. Perhaps empathy may help to close the gap. Before being too hasty and wanting to react negatively, pause and consider the bigger picture. On my website there are over 60 articles related to working with difficult people[82] that can offer you insights. These articles focus on a host of areas. In the end many difficult situations can be addressed early by building connecting relationships and listening actively. You are not out to make new friends with a bully, although that can happen. Rather, you are trying, at a minimum, to establish boundaries in order to have a frank discussion. Often the other party simply wants to be respected and be listened to. In mediation, neither party may leave feeling happy with the resolution. Rather, in successful mediations both parties can live with the solution. Sometimes that is the best possible conclusion.

Prevention of unfair tactics is often the best defense. When unfair tactics emerge, address those tactics head on. By addressing unfair tactics head on, this can serve to de-escalate tense situations. If you can't de-escalate and the situation blows up, take a break. Encourage both parties to stop, reflect, and see if it is possible to come back together—if not now, at a future date. Many times, referring back to the ground rules and the agenda can help opposing parties focus on why they are there. This can keep the negotiations going and remove distractions associated with derogatory behaviors. Here is a preschool example from a little girl that she recently shared this with me:

One day in preschool, Sara saw a boy in her class become angry and strike another child. The boy was scolded by the teacher and started crying. He was given a time out and told to go to a corner and stand there staring into the corner until he could stop crying and apologize to the child he had hit. Sara saw her classmate crying in the corner and walked up to him. "Are you okay?" she asked. "How are you feeling she asked?"

"I am angry and sad," said the boy through his tears.

"Do you want a hug?" Sara asked.

The boy looked up at her and stopped crying. With tears on his cheeks, he nodded slowly and said yes. Sara gave him a hug and the boy's face brightened. He left the corner and went over to apologize to the child he had hit. This is a true story told to me by Sara. Sara is only five, but she is wise beyond her years. She got it. We can learn from her.

The book *All I Really Need to Know I Learned in Kindergarten*[83] is full of stories that similarly can provide you insights on how to react towards others. It shows us that there is a different approach. Rather than coming down hard, focus on understanding. Coming down hard on difficult people can be counterproductive and often

> If we're hard on the problem and gentle on the people, we can create an opportunity to overcome conflict with empathy and point people towards collaboration.

does not solve the problem. If we're hard on the problem and gentle on the people, we can create an opportunity to overcome conflict with empathy and point people towards collaboration.

There are several types of negotiators[84] —a soft negotiator, a hard negotiator, and a principled negotiator—and each has distinctive tactics. The soft negotiator may make concessions in order to cultivate a relationship. A hard negotiator may demand concessions as a condition of a relationship. A principled negotiator will separate the people from the problem, focus on interests and create options. When a principled negotiator encounters the hard negotiator in a negotiation, the strategy is to require that both sides refocus on the problem. Do not be intimidated by the demands of a bullying approach. It is often quite successful to stand up to even an intimidating bully.

As a participant in a negotiation and as a leader it's always wise to begin with the end in mind. On the day when you receive a letter that indicates negotiations will be engaged, you should begin writing the final report. It will help you keep the issues in mind, and you will have some written material ready when you actually need to draft the final report. Plan your strategy and your anticipated close to a negotiation from the very beginning. Some elements may change during the process, but you will stay focused on the end goal. Negotiation is a process that must be well-thought-out and, at the same time, planned with multiple routes, leaving you flexible as the negotiation proceeds. Some negotiations are easy and require little thought. You can resolve these easily without much consideration. However, more complex conflicts and negotiations require a lot more preparation. In the course of this book a host of ideas have been presented relating to The Collaboration Effect. Now it is time to review them as you develop a more complete plan. Earlier in the book you were encouraged to develop a plan to improve the likelihood of success. It included the process of negotiation, which is a way of building a bridge towards closure in the negotiation. Here is a possible list of questions to remind you of the process.

- Why are we meeting?
- What do we hope to accomplish?
- Have we developed alternative positions between our starting position and our BATNA[85]?
- Who will participate?
- What are their roles?
- What would we want included in ground rules?
- When will we meet (time of day, day of week, duration of the session, multiple sessions)?
- Where will we have the meeting?
- How will we structure the meeting?
- Will there be an agenda and if there is who is preparing the agenda?
- What is our starting position?
- What are our interests economically, socially environmentally and emotionally?
- What do we think their interest are economically, socially, environmentally and emotionally?
- What do we see as the problem(s)?
- What alternatives do we want to propose?

- What alternatives do we think they may propose?
- How might we react to their proposals?
- What are the impacts of our and their potential proposals?
- How will we evaluate the alternatives?
- How will we demonstrate that we are listening to the other side?
- How do they know we care?
- Do we care if they care or not?
- How do we know if they care?
- Have we thought about and prepared our Best Alternative to Negotiated Agreement (BATNA[86]) if an agreement cannot be reached?

Has the process considered an absolute worst-case scenario—known as the Worst Alternative to a Negotiated Agreement (WATNA[87]) if an agreement cannot be reached? For example, might this mean that a company literally goes to war with a competitor or needs to file for bankruptcy? Such edge cases must be considered as possibilities. If the process moves toward such edge cases, a contingency plan must be created quickly.

Deadlines in the form of milestones and a terminal deadline are important. Consider your own list of milestone events and dates related to the negotiation so that you can bring these up and discuss them with the other side. Consider what the other side may propose ahead of time given your perspective. Then consider both sides with what might be appropriate milestones and deadlines that could lead to an amenable resolution resulting in closure. With these thoughts in mind here are some additional questions to consider.

- What will the schedule and timeline be for meetings?
- What deadlines need to be put in place?
- What if team members on our team or the other team do not meet these deadlines?
- What should be the penalties for missing deadlines?

- Who is the leader of this negotiation and how will he or she help the team stay focused and productive?
- What are the ground rules for the negotiating parties?

Significant movement in most straightforward negotiations takes place in the last 10% to 15% of the time set aside for the negotiation. For more complex negotiations or mediations, milestones are set with specific expectations.

In a negotiation with 12 issues amounting to more than $30 million in disputed claims, eight issues needed to be closed out in two days to address the other four issues over the course of another two days. Both parties had conceded that if an agreement was to be made then the first eight smaller issues in the first two days had to be agreed upon in order to proceed. Even if the last four issues were still not agreed upon, both parties would honor the agreement on those eight smaller issues if an agreement could be made on them in the first two days. Clear expectations matter in negotiations. They agreed to the first eight issues in the first two days and they proceeded to address the last four issues in the next two days. As a bullying technique, the negotiator on one side stated near the end of the fourth day when all but one issue was agreed that if the other side did not concede on this last issue, he was prepared to throw out all 12 issues. He was called out on this technique by the principled negotiator on the other side. This was not what they had agreed to as a matter of process and this would not be tolerated. That was that. The bullying technique was dispensed with and they collectively worked on the 12th and final issue timely to complete a successful negotiation. The key was to call out the bullying technique for what it was and not accept it by the other party. It worked.

Deadlines matter, too. In one of my negotiations, the parties spent an hour negotiating to extend the process for two hours. This occurred between boards of directors in two Fortune 100 companies, clear evidence that even such mundane issues exist at high levels. The players are inevitably all human and have similar frailties and faults no matter what their social or economic status. Yes, we spent an hour in a mediation to come to an agreement to extend the mediation process for two hours. Ironically, of course, the process only extended one hour of actual mediation time.

At times like this a break agreed to by both parties can sometimes be very helpful. Even though taking time out may seem counterproductive, often it can help in a negotiation. Sometimes providing for an extended recess from the process can help quell emotions. Many negotiations and some mediations go on for months, so breaks are inevitable. A month-long break may help the parties rethink their positions and develop creative, alternative, outside-the-box solutions that ultimately pave a route to closure. On smaller negotiations taking a short or even an extended break can make a big difference. This can help parties to calm down and come back with other productive ideas.

Penalties for late completions and missed deadlines can be useful, but they only address mistakes. Offering a bonus for work completed ahead of the deadline can provide an incentive for stakeholders to finish the tasks ahead of schedule. In addition, the ability to develop a good working relationship through incentives may induce positive, timely results not only in terms of deadlines, but also quality. It could also lead to future collaboration. Similarly, in a negotiation setting up a contingency in the negotiation can be very positive.

In some instances, there may be multiple negotiations going on at the same time. You may be negotiating with one party while an opposing party is negotiating with one of your competitors. You may have no idea how other negotiations are impacting the other party internally or externally. This is not unusual and can be quite distracting and tiresome for stakeholders on both sides of the table. One solution is to offer to have an exclusive negotiation with the opposing party for a limited period of time. Here is another situation where potentially a bonus incentive or some other type of sweetener may contribute to negotiating with you for an exclusive time period. By offering an exclusive negotiation you encourage the opposing party to focus on you and your concerns without distraction. This puts all the focus on your position and interests. Another potential issue that may arise is an impasse.

When parties find they are at an impasse, mediation[88] may offer an alternative to help all parties look beyond their positions and initial perspectives to find a reasonable range of outcomes. The first party may start at zero and the second party at 100. After initial opening statements, questions, and answers, the mediator encourages negotiations between the parties. As interests are clarified, facts shared, and additional insights uncovered, each of the parties moves off their starting position. Perhaps the first party eventually moves to 35% and the second party moves to 55%. This is their reasonable range. At this point there is a 20% difference between the parties.

Each party may have brought technical experts and attorneys to the mediation. The decision-makers may keep the mediator and the decision-makers in the room and ask everyone else to leave. At this point the decision-makers might typically discuss what might work to close the gap since they both want closure. In some cases, they may split the difference at this point. In other cases, new information may be provided by one side or the other to influence the outcome. Regardless, once two parties come to what each side determines to be a reasonable range, decision-makers move further off their positions for closure. To make this process work it is important to have the right mediator for the situation. Mediation is best when the mediator understands the type of issue and the mediator has extensive experience in that area in question before choosing a mediator. Explore what makes a good mediator[89]. Having had a good or bad experience in a recent negotiation or mediation may have an impact too.

Experts suggest that how we feel at the end of one negotiation can have a direct impact on the next negotiation—no matter whether the negotiation has ended positively or negatively. This **carryover effect** has been studied in various situations. and it has been documented[90] in a number of studies. Thus, it is important to identify and address our emotions before the next negotiation. If you had an accident on the way to work today, you would likely be distracted and be on edge throughout the day. From neuroscience, we know that if we lose our cool or experience trauma, specific chemicals and hormones are released in our body that stay in our blood stream for up to 22 hours or until we complete the next sleep cycle.[91] Such scenarios can happen in negotiations, too, and may extend over a longer period. A bad experience in our last negotiation may negatively impact our performance in subsequent negotiations. On the other hand, if we had a positive experience in our last negotiation, we may tend to be overconfident.

We also know that when attorneys are appointed to a mediation or negotiation, emotions like pride can impact outcomes. One study[92] of more than 4,500 cases found that 82 percent of the time a settlement offer was better than the actual court decision. Think about that for a moment. This means the attorney on one side or the other was given an offer to settle the case and rejected the offer, even though it was better than the eventual decision by the court. This means that attorneys could have settled the case without going to court and had a better outcome 82 percent of the time with their client.

There could be several reasons why the attorney and their client rejected the offer. Note that the attorney would receive a greater fee if the case went to court. Perhaps the attorney as a litigator preferred going to court and collecting a higher fee. The attorney may have confidently thought, we should not accept the offer because we will do better at trial. Maybe the client was so ingrained in his or her position that he or she refused to see a good offer when one was presented. Quite possibly the success or failure of the last case provided bias towards this case.

Understand that how well you negotiated your last negotiation will have an impact on the next one and so be receptive to alternatives and dampen your emotional instincts. The carryover effect might lead to false pride so remain humble even if you won the last time. If you lost, recognize that you may feel combative and focus on de-escalation. De-escalate[93] yourself and keep in mind the key elements of a negotiation as indicated below and carry them out relative to your negotiation.

Take breaks between negotiations. Don't schedule negotiations back to back. Give yourself time to either celebrate or heal. You don't want your emotions from one negotiation to impact the next negotiation. If you did well on the last negotiation, don't be over-confident going into the next one.

Practice the Seven Key Points for Negotiation

At the beginning of this book a story was presented. Recall the importance of conducting research on the parties ahead of time, providing an environment conducive to building a relationship, provide time for socialization and connecting relationships, focus on listening actively and being interested—not interesting, be humble and educate judiciously, explore areas of disagreement openly, and leave time for breaks, hydration and food. These are the major points to negotiate closure.

> **Prepare with Research**—Research the parties in advance on social media and network with others with the intention of engaging with the other party to build a connecting relationship. Reach out to the other party and ask something like "Since we will be working together if we could share some background on each other to simply get to know each other better, this may help the process. Would you be open to that?"

Provide a Relationship-Enhancing Environment— If it is possible to have a face to face meeting, find a pleasant, quiet, neutral location conducive to conversation. Provide relationship enhancing snacks, water, and beverages keyed to each party's preferences in advance. Provide a circular, trust-enhancing seating arrangement with only the key decision-makers present.

If it is not possible to have a face to face, physical meeting, explore an on-line meeting to allow for a visual observation of facial expressions and body language as well being able to listen to the words and tone of the conversation.

Begin with Socialization—Begin with small talk focusing on engaging the other parties on areas of interest based on your research and what you learned from your initial conversation. Focus on them and be clear of your genuine interest. Do not focus on yourself or try to be interesting. The key is let them do most of the talking. This is all about **connecting relationships**. If possible, have an engaging person present as a member of your team since basic human needs include food, water, shelter, and sex, and we want to appeal to them. After an appropriate period of time move into the business part of this meeting.

Be Curious and Listen Actively—Ask the other side about their position and the issues they want to discuss so that you can work with them to explore their interests. Try to determine how strongly they feel about the various issues. Work with the other side to develop an agenda on which issues will be addressed and in what order. Work to develop a time frame for discussion of the move into principal items if some seem more contentious than others. Once an agenda is determined, take on one issue at a time. For a given issue, listen actively. Take notes. Show and demonstrate empathy. Summarize, paraphrase, and demonstrate that you understand and care about their perspective. Ask open-ended questions. Attempt to summarize what you learned about their position on the issue, which may clarify it to the satisfaction of both of you. Show and demonstrate respect.

Be Humble and Educate Addressing Their Learning Styles—When it's your turn to talk, humbly educate the other side. Focus on the major points. Consider simple, engaging handouts. Candidly share your details via bullet points indicating your concerns and interests. **Educate judiciously.** Given what you hear from the other party, look for areas of agreement and celebrate those areas where collaboration can take place. Look for areas of agreement and point these out. Focus on building bridges to negotiate closure. Keep your eye on the prize. Avoid degenerating into negative commentary. Educate the other party in a way that is conducive to how the other party may best understand.

Explore Areas of Disagreement Openly— On areas of disagreement, consider reframing, re-examining, and re-engineering to explore other ways of looking at the issue. Consider generating other alternatives. Consider economic, environmental, and social implications of each alternative. Evaluate potential impacts. See if there may be a way to work collectively to address the issues. Be creative. Consider how employees, competitors, vendors, customers, and stakeholders may perceive any agreements. Explore other elements outside of the obvious that may have an impact on the issues (for example timing, quality, future contracts, long term relationships, and other important elements). Work collaboratively with the other party to address all interests.

Leave Time for Breaks, Restroom Time, Nutrition, and Hydration—Remember to follow a physical budget with ample time available for nutrition, timeouts, emotions, and bathroom breaks. In the end focus on doing the right thing, do what it takes and have fun along the way too.

Summary

This book is intended to demonstrate how The Collaboration Effect can help connect with others and negotiate at work and home. These strategies are to help you be more focused on the tasks at hand, have more control when navigating difficult decisions, engage in better strategies during negotiations, and find more peace in your professional and personal relationships.

You have learned the importance of collaboration and why you should practice these techniques both at work and home. Competition is important, but collaboration allows us to do even better. No one has all the right answers. Working together provides the possibility of a better outcome. The importance of people, technology, and information was emphasized. Make the effort to bring everyone on board. You and your team need to let go of the past and transition into the challenges and opportunities of the future. Yes, this is scary. Yes, this involves an element of chaos and risk, but it also involves the chance to be creative and adapt. This is an opportunity.

We need to prepare for such interactions with difficult people, so learn the techniques and apply them. Realize we won't always be successful. Mediation between parties can help calm the fire within to focus on the problem being hard on the problem and gentle on the people.

The Collaboration Effect provides an effective way to build trust. Its core ideas are about establishing connecting relationships, listening actively, and educating judiciously in order to build bridges to negotiate closure. Connecting relationships are those that engage with others after gaining their perspective. This requires effort to manage the relationship and to connect with others with whom we may need to negotiate, mediate, and/or facilitate going forward. Listening actively requires focusing on being interested instead of trying to be interesting. It involves paraphrasing, summarizing, asking open-ended questions, and empathizing with others. Communication is established through words, tone of voice, and facial and body language; it is often reciprocal with genuine conversation. Your attitude and appropriate enthusiasm to the situation are major elements in the process. By considering how the other party learns, humbly educate the other party to allow the other party to appreciate your perspective.

Finally, you learned how to build bridges to negotiate closure. You can identify and differentiate the who, where, when, what and how of negotiations.

As a final gift to you I have a de-escalation handout and a negotiation handout located on my website (www.mikegreg.com). I would be happy to give you a complimentary electronic copy of each. These references will come in handy when you find yourself in a negotiation and you want to remember key points to help you remain calm, to de-escalate yourself and others, and to set yourself up for success in a negotiation.

General George S. Patton, famous for his own arrogance, gained some insight about that over the course of his life, and wrote:

"The conquerors rode in a triumphal chariot... Sometimes his children robed in white stood with him in the chariot or rode the trace horses. A slave stood behind the conqueror holding a golden crown and whispering in his ear a warning: that all glory is fleeting."[94] Keep this in mind for yourself as you navigate successful negotiations. After a successful negotiation celebrate, but realize you have to start from scratch the next time regardless of your previous accomplishments. My hope is that this book has given you the tools to be inspired and successful when working with difficult people, overcoming conflict, and collaborating with others at work, at home, and in your broader community.

EPILOGUE

I n 1999 as an assistant director in a federal organization, I took
mediation training at Hamline University Law School (now
Mitchell Hamline School of Law) in St. Paul, Minnesota. When
I returned from training, my director asked me to mediate a budget issue between two division chiefs. They were at a major budget impasse. It was a baptism by fire, but the tactics I had learned
resolved the issue. My director could not believe it, and I was grate-
ful. After that, he had me apply my skills in a number of areas in
the district related to labor management, equal employment opportunity (EEO), administrative issues, and other matters in dispute.

A few months later, I was sent to another part of the coun-
try to be acting assistant director for five months. After a week of
doing my regular job, I said to the director that I could see several areas where I believed systems needed to be reviewed, and I
recommended training all managers in mediation. He concurred
and I regularly briefed the director on the progress with the Equal
Employment Opportunity (EEO) office, labor relations, human
resources, the division chiefs, middle managers, front line managers, and the union.

To make a long story short, in five months the number of official conflicts was reduced from more than 300 to fewer than 30.
When a short-term acting assistant director leaves there is a tradi-
tional coffee farewell event. Normally about 15 to 20 people stop by
and it lasts for about an hour. Some come to be seen by the director,

and others are friends made during the acting assignment. That day more than 400 of the 1,200 employees came, and it took me over six hours to shake their hands. This moved me greatly, and changed my life forever. To be clear, I was not the hero. The hero is the change in processes and the implementation of conflict resolution, which I have now tried to share with my program, The Collaboration Effect. It's not about me. It's all about we. But we starts with me. What is satisfying to me is to share this process with you so that you too can have more constructive and peaceful resolutions based on this system I developed over the years. It can work for you too. Building connecting relationships, listening actively, and educating judiciously leads to building bridges to negotiate closure. The process (The Collaboration Effect) is the real hero. Now that you have read this book, you too know the not-so-secret framework and can apply the process at work, and home. You can take it from here. Good luck. God bless and blessed are the peacemakers.

ENDNOTES

1   http://erikagarms.com/creating-brain-friendly-workplaces/

2   blueberries, almonds, carrot sticks, celery sticks, cut up fruit, dark chocolate and peanut butter.

3   https://www.jneurosci.org/content/34/47/15621
https://www.ncbi.nlm.nih.gov/pmc/articles/PMC4752429/
https://www.ncbi.nlm.nih.gov/pmc/articles/PMC2948535/

4   https://www.brookings.edu/blog/education-plus-development/2017/12/12/complementary-strategies-for-teaching-collaboration-and-critical-thinking-skills/

5   https://www.mikegreg.com/blog/way-enhance-your-reputation-bargaining-table#sthash.S147QpTJ.dpbs

6   https://insidebigdata.com/2017/11/10/top-skills-needed-thrive-ai-economy/

7   https://independentsector.org/resource/why-diversity-equity-and-inclusion-matter/
https://ideal.com/diversity-and-inclusion/
https://jermainedavis.com/product/be-diversity-competent/
https://www.amazon.com/gp/product/B01LY9G3VY/ref=dbs_a_def_rwt_hsch_vapi_tkin_p1_i3

8   https://mikegreg.com/blog/how-can-you-foster-inclusion-work

9   https://conference.iste.org/uploads/ISTE2016/HANDOUTS/KEY_100525149/understandingtheSCARFmodel.pdf

10 https://biz30.timedoctor.com/virtual-team-building/
11 https://www.mindtools.com/pages/article/newPPM_87.htm
12 https://www.mikegreg.com/blog/what-batna-and-how-can-you-use-negotiation-especially-difficult-people
13 https://www.mikegreg.com/blog/ten-steps-interest-based-resolution
14 https://www.esri.com/about/newsroom/arcuser/a-seven-step-strategy-for-managing-technology-change/
15 https://www.changefactory.com.au/our-thinking/articles/managing-change-in-information-management/
16 https://www.amazon.com/Servant-Manager-Michael-Gregory/dp/0986030740/ref=sr_1_1?ie=UTF8&qid=153992 4580&sr=8-1&keywords=the%20servant%20 manager Tip 42 Provide Feedforward for Results
17 https://www.mikegreg.com/blog/negotiations-brain-and-stress-part-i#sthash.HyJvzwhL.dpbs
18 https://www.mikegreg.com/blog/how-actively-listen-negotiation
19 https://www.mikegreg.com/blog/what-does-trust-have-do-collaboration-effect-%C2%AE
20 https://mikegreg.com/peaceful-resolutions
21 https://www.mikegreg.com/blog/what-you-tell-yourself-matters-difficult-people-and-situations#sthash.o4CGKI4D.dpbs
22 https://blog.hubspot.com/sales/the-art-of-asking-open-ended-questions
23 https://effectiviology.com/self-distancing-rational-decisions/
24 https://greatergood.berkeley.edu/article/item/four_ways_to_gain_perspective_on_negative_events
25 http://selfcontrol.psych.lsa.umich.edu/wp-content/uploads/2017/04/SD.pdf
26 https://www.inc.com/scott-mautz/5-ways-emotionally-intelligent-people-stay-calm-in-heat-of-moment-according-to-science.html

27 https://www.mikegreg.com/blog/how-manage-conflict

28 https://sharpbrains.com/blog/2006/10/22/is-there-such-thing-as-good-stress/#:~:text=We%20all%20need%20some%20stress,a%20release%20can%20cause%20damage.

29 https://www.mikegreg.com/blog/take-advantage-collaboration-effect-%E2%80%93-relationships

30 https://www.mikegreg.com/blog/how-actively-listen-negotiation

31 https://mikegreg.com/blog/educate-judiciously-take-advantage-collaboration-effect

32 https://mikegreg.com/blog/how-close-deal-negotiation-1

33 https://greatergood.berkeley.edu/topic/social_connection/definition

34 https://greatergood.berkeley.edu/search?q=active+listening+and+neuroscience
https://greatergood.berkeley.edu/images/application_uploads/Teaching_empathy.pdf

35 https://greatergood.berkeley.edu/article/item/nine_things_educators_need_to_know_about_the_brain
https://www.tandfonline.com/doi/full/10.1080/23735082.2019.1685027

36 https://www.google.com/search?source=hp&ei=Q3FUXfPnG7qO9PwPsOeBgA0&q=why+is+trust+important&oq=why+is+trust+important&gs_l=psy-ab.3..0l10.328.4700..7977...2.0..1.282.2081.23j1j1......0....1..gws-wiz.......0i131j0i10.G-Hc4UghvdU&ved=0ahUKEwizlY7qm4PkAhU6B50JHbBzANAQ4dUDCAc&uact=5

37 https://www.mikegreg.com/blog/what-does-trust-have-do-collaboration-effect-%C2%AE

38 https://www.amazon.com/Servant-Manager-Michael-Gregory/dp/0986030740
https://www.amazon.com/Trust-Edge-Leaders-Relationships-Stronger/dp/1476711372

39 https://www.td.org/insights/the-neuroscience-of-leadership-and-trust

40 https://www.livescience.com/42198-what-is-oxytocin.html#:~:text=Oxytocin%20is%20a%20hormone%20secreted,snuggle%20up%20or%20bond%20socially.

41 The Servant Manager Tip 73 https://www.amazon.com/Servant-Manager-Michael-Gregory/dp/0986030740/ref=sr_1_1?ie=UTF8&qid=1539924580&sr=8-1&keywords=the%20servant%20manager

42 https://www.pon.harvard.edu/daily/business-negotiations/small-talk-big-gains/

43 https://www.forbes.com/sites/frankarmstrong/2019/10/21/trust-but-verify/#6bc1d0d05873

44 https://www.pon.harvard.edu/daily/mediation/types-mediation-choose-type-best-suited-conflict/

45 https://www.amazon.com/Peaceful-Resolutions-Illustrated-Conflict-Resolution-ebook/dp/B01N5D065X/ref=sr_1_1?ie=UTF8&qid=1539924496&sr=8-1&keywords=peaceful%20resolutions

46 https://www.mikegreg.com/blog/how-actively-listen-negotiation

47 https://www.mikegreg.com/blog/how-listen-better-difficult-people

48 https://bookmarklee.co.uk/three-elements-of-communication-and-the-so-called-7-38-55-rule/

49 https://www.mikegreg.com/blog/five-dispute-resolution-skills-help-you

50 https://www.mikegreg.com/categories/mindfulness-meditation-and-health

51 https://www.mindful.org/10-things-we-know-about-the-science-of-meditation/

52 https://greatergood.berkeley.edu/article/item/a_little_meditation_goes_a_long_way#:~:text=The%20study%2C%20published%20last%20month,memory%2C%20stress%2C%20and%20empathy.

53 https://www.ncbi.nlm.nih.gov/pmc/articles/PMC3303565/#:~:text=Meditation%20techniques%20appear%20to%20produce,systolic%20and%20diastolic%20blood%20pressure.

54 https://www.mindful.org/meditation-anxious-emotions/

55 https://mindworks.org/blog/long-term-benefits-of-meditation/

56 https://greatergood.berkeley.edu/video/item/how_to_protect_your_body_from_social_media_stress

57 https://greatergood.berkeley.edu/article/item/better_than_sex_and_appropriate_for_kids

58 https://greatergood.berkeley.edu/tag/mindfulness+meditation/rh

59 https://www.cnn.com/2020/03/23/health/yale-happiness-course-wellness/index.html

60 https://www.mikegreg.com/blog/shift-how-you-think-about-confrontations-impact-outcome

61 https://www.pon.harvard.edu/daily/international-negotiation-daily/bridging-the-cultural-divide-in-international-business-negotiations/

62 https://www.mikegreg.com/blog/how-win-negotiation-preparation

63 https://www.pon.harvard.edu/uncategorized/negotiation-preparation-checklist/?utm_source=WhatCountsEmail&utm_medium=daily&utm_date=2019-04-23-13-30-00&mqsc=E4048692

64 https://www.mikegreg.com/blog/validate-other-side

65 http://thescienceexplorer.com/brain-and-body/neuroscience-tips-remain-calm-argument

66 https://www.mikegreg.com/blog/how-win-negotiation-preparation

67 https://andreasamadi.podbean.com/e/the-neuroscience-of-personal-change/
68 https://collabeffect.com/conflict-resolution-when-core-values-are-involved/
69 https://www.myrkothum.com/personal-strengths-and-weaknesses/
70 https://leadershiplifesupport.com/know-your-strengths-weaknesses/
and
https://journeytoleadershipblog.com/2017/05/06/identify-strengths-weaknesses-work-importance/
71 https://www.mbtionline.com/
72 https://www.thoughtco.com/three-different-learning-styles-3212040
73 http://www.nollassociates.com/
Neuropsychology%20of%20Conflict.pdf
74 https://www.theaskingformula.com/john-baker/
75 https://en.wikipedia.org/wiki/Pareto_principle
76 https://en.wikipedia.org/wiki/Rule_of_three_(writing)
77 https://www.amazon.com/Peaceful-Resolutions-Illustrated-Conflict-Resolution-ebook/dp/B01N5D065X/ref=sr_1_1?ie
=UTF8&qid=1539924496&sr=8-1&keywords=
peaceful%20resolutions
https://www.amazon.com/Getting-Yes-Negotiating-Agreement-Without/dp/0143118757
https://www.amazon.com/Getting-Past-Negotiating-Difficult-Situations/dp/0553371312/ref=pd_lpo_14_img_
1/131-8334809-6242115?_encoding=UTF8&pd_rd_i=
0553371312&pd_rd_r=835792ec-a78c-4b58-9003-
4802f603f4c9&pd_rd_w=M3zbE&pd_rd_wg=I9lNA&pf_
rd_p=7b36d496-f366-4631-94d3-61b87b52511b&pf_rd_
r=YJQH6KTDJ65ZZ1PN9385&psc=1&refRID=YJQH6K
TDJ65ZZ1PN9385

78 https://www.amazon.com/Peaceful-Resolutions-Michael-Gregory/dp/1945148004

79 https://www.mikegreg.com/blog/what-anchor-negotiation-why-does-it-matter

80 https://en.wikipedia.org/wiki/Anchoring_(cognitive_bias)

81 https://mikegreg.com/blog/dealing-difficult-people

82 https://www.mikegreg.com/blog/11

83 https://en.wikipedia.org/wiki/All_I_Really_Need_to_Know_I_Learned_in_Kindergarten

84 https://www.amazon.com/Peaceful-Resolutions-Michael-Gregory/dp/1945148004

85 https://www.pon.harvard.edu/daily/batna/translate-your-batna-to-the-current-deal/

86 https://www.pon.harvard.edu/daily/batna/translate-your-batna-to-the-current-deal/

87 https://www.pon.harvard.edu/tag/watna/

88 https://www.mikegreg.com/blog/mediation-process-business-negotiations#sthash.3jvPzn5d.dpbs

89 https://www.mikegreg.com/blog/what-questions-should-you-ask-about-dispute-resolution#sthash.HEIelPst.dpbs

90 https://www.pon.harvard.edu/daily/dealmaking-daily/closing-deal-negotiations-3-tips-sequential-dealmaking/?mqsc=E3917295

91 Neurologist Dr. Erika Garms presentation on Building Brain Friendly Workplaces to EBITDA Partners, Roseville, MN August 3, 2017

92 https://www.scribd.com/document/369545878/Kiser-Study

93 https://www.scribd.com/document/368337579/De-Escalation-Handout

94 https://www.goodreads.com/quotes/632929-for-over-a-thousand-years-roman-conquerors-returning-from-the

www.ingramcontent.com/pod-product-compliance
Lightning Source LLC
Chambersburg PA
CBHW071706210326
41597CB00017B/2363